Withdrawn

MASTERS AT WORK

BECOMING A NEUROSURGEON

BECOMING A VETERINARIAN

BECOMING A VENTURE CAPITALIST

BECOMING A HAIRSTYLIST

BECOMING A REAL ESTATE AGENT

BECOMING A MARINE BIOLOGIST

BECOMING AN ETHICAL HACKER

BECOMING A LIFE COACH

BECOMING A YOGA INSTRUCTOR

BECOMING A RESTAURATEUR

BECOMING A PRIVATE INVESTIGATOR

BECOMING A BAKER

MASTERS AT WORK

BECOMING A MIDWIFE

SANDI DOUGHTON

SIMON & SCHUSTER

New York London Toronto Sydney New Delhi

Simon & Schuster
1230 Avenue of the Americas
New York, NY 10020

Names and other identifying information of some of the patients
profiled in this book have been changed to protect their privacy.
Patients' actual names are used only if I have received permission to do so.

First Simon & Schuster hardcover edition December 2020

For information about special discounts for bulk purchases,
please contact Simon & Schuster Special Sales at 1-866-506-1949
or business@simonandschuster.com.

The Simon & Schuster Speakers Bureau can bring authors to your live event. For
more information or to book an event, contact the Simon & Schuster Speakers Bureau
at 1-866-248-3049 or visit our website at www.simonspeakers.com.

Illustrations by Donna Mehalko

Manufactured in the United States of America

1   3   5   7   9   10   8   6   4   2

Library of Congress Cataloging-in-Publication Data

Names: Doughton, Sandi, author.
Title: Becoming a midwife / Sandi Doughton.
Description: First Simon & Schuster hardcover edition. | New York : Simon & Schuster,
2020. | Series: Masters at work | Includes bibliographical references. |
Identifiers: LCCN 2020032861 (print) | LCCN 2020032862 (ebook) | ISBN
9781982141431 (hardcover) | ISBN 9781982141448 (ebook)
Subjects: LCSH: Kopas, Mary Lou. | University of Washington. Medical Center. |
Midwives—Washington (State)—Seattle. | Midwives—Washington (State)—Seattle—
Biography. | Midwifery—Vocational guidance—United States.
Classification: LCC RG962.S43 D68 2020 (print) | LCC RG962.S43 (ebook) | DDC
618.2009797/772—dc23
LC record available at https://lccn.loc.gov/2020032861
LC ebook record available at https://lccn.loc.gov/2020032862

ISBN 978-1-9821-4143-1
ISBN 978-1-9821-4144-8 (ebook)

For my mother, Jo Anne Koehler—
I don't know how you did it, but you did.

CONTENTS

By the time the call comes in at 2:30 p.m., Mary Lou Kopas has already helped three women give birth.

The first was Monique, at 8:30 a.m. Aided by an anesthetic called an epidural, she pushed for a scant half hour after her water broke before delivering her second child into Kopas's hands. The little girl needed a few puffs from a neonatal respirator to boost her breathing but now is nursing with gusto.

Next was Sofia, who had hoped for an unmedicated birth until three days of labor left her ragged and exhausted. She opted for an epidural, which allowed her to sleep for a few hours. The delivery went fine, but a bit of placenta refused to detach from the uterus. Kopas couldn't dislodge it, nor could the obstetrician she called for assistance. Facing the risk of hemorrhage, the new mother was whisked to the operating room, where Kopas helped the surgeon perform a procedure to remove tissue from the uterus called a D&C: dilation and curettage.

Then came Nayantara. After four hours of labor, she delivered her first child, a boy, without pain medication. "That one was very nice," Kopas says, smiling. "The baby just glided out."

Back-to-back-to-back babies aren't the normal order of business at University of Washington Medical Center–Northwest, where Kopas leads a team of six certified nurse-midwives. "I might get a day this busy once a year," she says, plopping into a chair after the third birth—and just before the phone rings.

On the line is Amie-June Brumble, a thirty-seven-year-old law firm supervisor nearing the due date for her second child. She tells Kopas she's been having sporadic contractions since early morning but isn't sure whether they signal the start of active labor.

Kopas hasn't eaten anything but a handful of hazelnuts since breakfast. She's barely had time to pee. But as she chats with the expectant mother, her voice is unhurried and calm. There's no hint of stress, no indication she has been running nonstop for nearly eight hours. "The patient doesn't care how busy you are," Kopas explains later. "Your job is to be there for her, to give her your full attention."

In that way, midwifery has changed little from its ancient roots. Derived from Old English, the word *midwife* means "with woman." Centuries later, that's still how Kopas defines her basic commitment to patients: "It means being there with her no matter what happens."

Following in the footsteps of midwives through the ages, Kopas helps women navigate the joys, terrors, and transformations of pregnancy and birth—experiences that rank among humanity's most primal. But midwifery today is backed by the power of modern medicine. While midwives of old had no formal training and helped women deliver at home, nurse-midwives like Kopas are highly educated professionals who work mostly in hospitals. They offer their patients the personalized, holistic care that is the hallmark of midwifery—and the peace of mind that comes from knowing surgeons and state-of-the-art resources are close at hand if needed.

That's why Brumble chose the UW midwives for both her pregnancies. She knew she didn't want a typical hospital experience, with bright lights and medical staff rushing in and out and an obstetrician she might never have met before. She wanted to see if she could give birth naturally, with no pressure from busy doctors to speed up her labor or dull the pain with drugs.

"I didn't want to be treated as a medical emergency," Brumble explained during a prenatal checkup with Kopas two weeks earlier. "I felt that this was an experience that has been common to women, of women and for women throughout our species' history, and I wanted to have a more personal connection with it." But she also wanted quick access to medical care if anything went wrong.

Now, on the phone with Kopas, she describes contractions that started off mild and irregular but have been getting stronger and closer together. Before her first son's birth three and a half years ago, Brumble and her husband packed a bag with fuzzy slippers, music, and snacks to help her through labor. But the baby came so fast they barely made it to the hospital in time. The bag sat in the car, forgotten, until long after the birth. Brumble doesn't want to repeat that experience, but she's wary of jumping the gun. And, she tells Kopas, she's not sure her insurance will cover a hospital visit for a false alarm.

"Could you be at the clinic by three thirty?" Kopas asks. "I could buzz over there and check you out."

The UW Medical Center–Northwest Midwives Clinic

in North Seattle, a few blocks from the hospital, is where Kopas and her colleagues have their offices and conduct patient exams. Since she doesn't have any more women in labor at the moment, Kopas has time to dash to the clinic, where there will be no question about insurance coverage.

But first, there's record keeping to catch up on. Kopas clicks open a screen on her computer. Reading glasses perched on her nose, she quickly types in the details of Nayantara's delivery, along with orders for a handful of drugs and other palliatives to ease postpartum discomfort: ibuprofen, laxatives, witch hazel pads to soothe tender tissues. "You always have to chart what you're doing, and you can't get too far behind," she says.

Kopas is dressed in blue scrubs, her standard uniform for hospital shifts. Her graying hair is pulled up and clipped but keeps falling around her face. On her right forearm is a tattoo of a female elephant and calf. The matriarchal mammals, who tend each other's births and rush to the aid of babies in distress, are a kind of totem for Kopas. At fifty-four, she's approaching matriarch status herself as a leading advocate—and agitator—for women's health in Washington State.

One of her inspirations was the badass midwife who helped her teenage sister through pregnancy and birth in the early 1980s, a time when out-of-wedlock babies were still considered scandalous by some—including Kopas's Catholic parents. Her sister described the midwife striding down the hall of the small hospital in western Massachusetts wearing knee-high suede boots with tassels and drawing incredulous stares from doctors and nurses. "She was the rebel in the hospital," Kopas recalls. "That's what planted the seed for me."

With her computer work done, Kopas checks her watch. There's just enough time to grab a bite. She navigates the hospital cafeteria with the dexterity of a person used to eating on the fly, snatching a sandwich and hummus, then heading for her car. En route to the clinic, she points out a favorite cotton shopping bag in the back seat, decorated with a silhouette of jagged peaks, the phases of the moon, and the message "Menses Move Mountains."

At the clinic, Kopas wolfs down the sandwich while conferring with a colleague about another patient. When Brumble and her husband, Tyler, arrive, the clinic nurse leads them to an exam room. Wearing a long gray skirt and a blue tee shirt, Brumble lumbers slowly down the hall, with Tyler at her elbow. The nurse straps a fetal heart monitor around the pregnant woman's belly and helps her onto the table.

Kopas greets the couple and asks how they're holding up. Lying on her side and holding Tyler's hand, Brumble explains that her contractions got stronger and closer together during the ride to the clinic. Her wavy blond hair hangs loose around her shoulders. Tyler's brown hair is equally long and twisted into a braid. Brumble grimaces and screws her eyes shut as a contraction pulses through her body. "Yes, yes, yes," she chants under her breath, rocking and tightening her grip on her husband's hand. When the pain passes, she opens her eyes and exhales.

Kopas examines the readout on the monitor. "The heart rate looks fine," she says. "There's nothing worrisome in there."

Kopas pulls on surgical gloves and asks Brumble to scoot to the edge of the table. During the first stage of labor, the cervix, or neck of the uterus, thins and gradually opens to accommodate the baby's passage. The extent of thinning—called effacement—and dilation are landmarks that map a woman's progression toward delivery. Kopas can't see the cervix, so she bridges the opening with two fingers and estimates. It's a skill that takes time to master. Misjudging the size of the cervical opening is a typical rookie mistake for new midwives.

Brumble is at four centimeters, about the diameter of a Ritz cracker. That's a little less than halfway to the all-systems-go maximum of ten centimeters, and wide enough to signal active labor.

Since Brumble's first birth was a lightning-fast affair and second babies often come quicker, Kopas suggests the couple head for the hospital.

"You're ready. You can do this," she says. "My money is on sometime in the next few hours."

No one takes the bet. If they had, Kopas would have won.

Soon after the couple settles into their birthing suite, Brumble's contractions intensify. Now dressed in a green, open-backed gown, with her hair pulled away from her face and braided, she leans over the bed, squeezing a pillow and groaning. Her toes curl with each contraction. Kopas rubs her back, while Tyler fans her flushed neck.

Natural labor is a spontaneous process triggered by an interplay of signals from the mother, fetus, and placenta. Powerful and primordial, it commandeers a woman's body and doesn't let go until the birth is complete. For some women, contractions are not much worse than severe menstrual cramps. Others describe labor as the most agonizing experience of their lives. "I begged my hubby to throw me out of the car on the way to the hospital, it hurt so bad," one woman writes. "I really thought my muscles were going to tear apart," says another.

By the time Brumble got to the hospital for her first son's birth, the pain was so overwhelming she briefly considered giving up on natural childbirth. But it was too late for an epidural, which is injected into the space around the spinal cord. This time, her early labor was light. She was able to work at home, taking care of chores and getting the house ready for the baby. As she arrived at the hospital, she was still chatting and joking. Now all she can do is lower her head and groan, a low, throaty sound like a rumbling bear.

When the contraction eases, she rises to pace the room. The next wave takes hold and Brumble leans against her husband. Head to head as if slow dancing, the couple sway to the internal rhythms moving their son closer to birth.

Kopas stands back, watchful but not intruding on the intimate moments.

She's the medical authority in the room, the person who holds two lives in her hands and directs a team that includes a labor nurse and a neonatal nurse. It's the same top-dog position the obstetrician occupies in most hospital births. Barring any complications that require a doctor's assistance, Kopas will be the one in charge throughout, overseeing both Brumble's care and the baby's.

The bedrock tenet of midwifery is that birth is a natural process. It's not a sickness. It's not a pathological condition. Midwives intervene only when needed or wanted. Women are free to labor any way—and pretty much anywhere—they feel comfortable: in a tub, walking the halls, lying on the floor, or curled up in a chair. Every midwife has stories of babies born atop a toilet, or in a doorway or corridor.

Midwives often describe their job as "catching babies." It's a charming phrase that honors the mother for doing the hard work of delivery. But it doesn't really reflect the complexity of the midwife's role—which includes being constantly alert for trouble. During labor, Kopas needs to ensure that the forces roiling the mother's body aren't harming the baby. If the umbilical cord is compressed, it can strangle the oxygen supply. The placenta sometimes tears away from the uterine wall prematurely. Complications like that are rare and unlikely for a woman like Brumble with no risk factors. But Kopas doesn't assume. She asks the labor nurse to periodically check the baby's heart rate with a handheld ultrasound device called a Doppler. Pressed to Brumble's belly, the instrument amplifies watery thumps that pound away at a robust 150 beats per minute.

Another key part of the midwife's job is to gauge the level of support and encouragement each woman needs. For first-time moms climbing the walls with anxiety, Kopas does whatever seems to help—holding their hands, gazing into their eyes, helping them count and breathe and focus. Some women enter a Zen-like state and don't want anything to break the spell. As Brumble's pain builds, Kopas begins to murmur words of encouragement. The laboring woman is back on the bed, curled on her side. Kopas massages her back through a minute-long contraction. She presses a cool washcloth to Brumble's neck and urges her to catch her breath and rest when the grip relaxes.

"I forgot why this was a good idea," Brumble says, gasping.

"Because babies are so cute and cuddly," Kopas says, rubbing her feet. "And when they come, labor is over."

"Oh, God. Oh, God," Brumble moans, almost sobbing. "I think I'm ready to start pushing."

In most hospital births, this is the point when the lights are cranked up and the obstetrician—who usually isn't present throughout labor—is called back into the room. She or he will maneuver the woman onto her back and into stirrups, then reach into her vagina to confirm that the cervix is fully dilated. If it is, the doctor will often start instructing the woman like a drill sergeant, telling her when to push and for how long.

Kopas does none of that. She and the nurses move quietly, making their final preparations. The labor nurse wheels in a cart of instruments covered with a blue drape. The neonatal nurse tests the respirator she will use if the baby has any trouble breathing. Kopas pulls on a pair of gloves and asks Brumble what position she prefers.

Hands and knees, Brumble replies.

The nurses wrestle a horseshoe-shaped pillow onto the bed and help Brumble turn so it supports her upper body.

Kopas leans in and pats Brumble's hand. "You ready?" she asks. "Start taking deep breaths. Blow it out, all the way down to the baby."

Brumble growls, then roars as she pushes into the next contraction. Standing next to the bed, Kopas presses down on her patient's lower back to alleviate the pressure.

"Stay with it," she urges.

Brumble grips the head of the bed and screams. Raw and wild, the sound pours out of her and fills the room. A gush of liquid floods the bed.

"Your bag of water just broke," Kopas says. Brumble lets out a rush of air, half panting, half crying. Kopas positions herself between Brumble's legs. "We're getting so close now. Just listen to your body," she urges.

Brumble groans and pushes and pushes and groans.

Kopas leans in again, her head next to Brumble's. "Amie-June," she says emphatically, to penetrate the fog. "You're so close. You can do this. We're all with you."

"It hurts," Brumble says, almost whispering.

"I know," Kopas says, softly now. "You're doing so well. You're doing amazing. You got this."

Kopas peers at Brumble's bottom. She cups the vagina with her hand, feeling the bulge of the baby's head.

"Can you see anything?" Brumble asks.

"No, but I can feel him."

Another push, and the top of the head appears.

"Now I can see him," Kopas says. "Little pushes! Little pushes!"

Then suddenly, another person is in the room.

Smeared and bloody, trailing a milky-blue cord, a tiny body fills Kopas's hands. Only seconds old, the new human knows what to do. His mouth flies open. Pulling breath into lungs that have never before filled with air, he begins to cry.

"You did it, Amie-June!" Kopas exclaims. "So beautiful."

Naked and trembling, Brumble tucks her legs beneath her and rocks onto her haunches.

"Here's your baby," Kopas says, passing the flailing bundle to his mother, who clasps him to her chest and gazes into his face.

"Oh," she breathes. "Hi."

2

Neither Kopas's nor Brumble's work is done.

With the baby sprawled across her body, the new mother alternately sobs and laughs and draws her husband close. A little more than two hours have passed since they arrived at the hospital. Time elapsed between Brumble's water breaking and birth: nine minutes.

"That was fast," Kopas says.

"That's how I do it," Brumble replies, her sense of humor returning.

The neonatal nurse places a cap on the baby's head, swabs him with soft cloths, and covers him with blankets. Glancing at her notes, she realizes no one has confirmed the sex.

"Did you see boy parts?' she asks Kopas, who chuckles and does a quick crotch check.

"The important thing is that he's breathing," Kopas says. "He's pink. He cried as soon as he came out: it doesn't get any better than that."

Kopas doesn't rush to clamp the umbilical cord, a practice that until recently was routine in most births with obstetricians. Speed is only necessary if the newborn is entangled or needs resuscitation. Midwives have long advocated delayed clamping because blood from the placenta can help inflate the newborn's lungs and continue providing nourishment and oxygen for several minutes. Benefits to the baby's iron level can last for months. When the cord finally stops pulsing, Kopas clamps it and hands her scissors to Tyler.

"There's no going back now, son," she murmurs to the squirming infant as his dad makes the snip. "You're on your own."

Kopas palpates Brumble's abdomen, checking to see if her uterus is contracting and preparing to expel the placenta. "Can you give a little push?" she asks.

The slab of tissue that has been the baby's lifeline for the past thirty-eight-and-a-half weeks slides out easily. Kopas examines it to ensure no chunks are missing. Delivering the placenta can be a perilous time for women. As it shears away from the uterus, the dense web of veins and arteries that shuttle blood between the mother and fetus is severed and the risk of postpartum hemorrhage is highest.

Kopas offers Brumble a dose of Pitocin, a drug that causes

the uterus to contract and helps reduce bleeding. In typical hospital births, drugs are often administered as a matter of course with little or no discussion. Except in emergencies— and even then, when possible—midwives ask and explain and offer advice. The decision is the woman's.

Brumble agrees to the shot. "I like not hemorrhaging," she says.

When Kopas urged small pushes just before the baby made his exit, she was hoping to ease the head slowly through the vaginal opening and give the tissues a chance to stretch. But things happened so quickly Brumble was left with a second-degree tear in the skin and muscles of her vagina and perineum—a common injury in childbirth. As Kopas prepares to suture it, the nurse rolls in a surgical lamp and helps the midwife slip a fresh gown over her scrubs.

Kopas pulls up a stool and sits between Brumble's legs, probing the delicate tissue gently with her gloved finger. After enduring labor and childbirth with no drugs, Brumble also declines nitrous oxide gas—a mild painkiller. Kopas instead dabs on lidocaine, a topical anesthetic, and waits for it to kick in. Brumble grimaces with pain at the first needle poke.

Reading glasses back on her nose, Kopas works quickly

and carefully to get the uncomfortable task done. When she finishes, she presses on Brumble's belly to check her uterus again. "Did any blood come out?" the midwife asks. The answer is no. "The stitches dissolve," Kopas explains. "Ice feels good. It will feel better day to day."

Kopas bundles up the wet, bloody cloths and pads from the bed—an action that seems casual but can also be an important part of postpartum care. Since the dry weight of each cloth is known, blood loss can be quantified by weighing them after they've served their function.

As Kopas cleans up, the nurses help the new mother get back in her gown and tucked into bed. Tyler at her side, Brumble nudges the baby toward her breast.

The atmosphere in the room shifts subtly. With the hard part over and both mother and baby doing well, Kopas and the nurses seem to pause and soak in the aura of love and contentment that radiates from the new family. The only person who isn't smiling is the newborn intent on finding a nipple.

Kopas has been in the birth business for more than fifteen years. She estimates she's been present at more than six hundred deliveries, first as an obstetrical nurse and now as a midwife. Yet there's nothing to suggest this is just another

day at the office for her. She beams as if she has never witnessed a more wondrous scene than Brumble and her husband and the tiny, wrinkled being they just brought into
the world.

That's what being a midwife is all about, Kopas says, after
slipping quietly from the room. Her aim is to help women
birth their babies in a way that's safe and leaves them feeling empowered and joyful—not bulldozed by a system that

often shows little regard for their wishes. Sometimes that means Kopas will advise a woman to induce labor, accept an epidural, or even agree to a C-section when it's best for her and the baby. Sometimes it means offering little more than encouragement and vigilance while a woman like Brumble gives birth mostly on her own.

"When you see a woman go through unmedicated labor, it's a powerful thing," Kopas says. "You know how much she's enduring, and the fact that she's dealing with it without screaming for pain medicine—it's amazing.

"If that's not moving to me—if I don't feel like I can get teary-eyed at most every birth—I'm probably in the wrong business."

IT TOOK KOPAS A long time to figure out midwifery was the right business for her. Growing up with feminist values, she disdained traditional women's occupations for their often subservient status, nursing most of all. Nor was she drawn to medicine, which struck her as lacking in creativity. Her passion was for research and discovery. She delved into oceanography and marine science, then detoured into environmental activism. By the time she zeroed in on midwifery as a career, life intervened. She paused to raise two sons while slowly easing her way into the profession via—yes—nursing.

"If they'd still had the stupid little caps, I wouldn't have been able to do it," she says.

Nearly fifteen years passed between the time Kopas decided to become a midwife and her graduation from the University of Washington's midwifery program. But it didn't take her long to become a leader in a state with a robust community of practitioners and some of the country's best policies for midwives.

Roundabout routes like Kopas's aren't uncommon in the field. Medical professionals, including many nurses, switch to midwifery after becoming disillusioned with mainstream maternity care. Others are inspired by their own birth experiences—both good and harrowing. Some people are drawn to the profession as a way to correct racial and social disparities in maternal and newborn health or reach underserved communities. Whatever the motivation, midwifery is not a career anyone stumbles into. It's a calling.

Many Americans have no idea the profession still exists outside religious communities and off-the-grid enclaves. Kopas had never heard of midwifery before her sister's experience. "We're a little-known secret," she says.

The number of schools that offer training is limited. The education is costly and financial aid is scarce. Midwives who work in hospitals can feel marginalized in a country where 90 percent of women choose to give birth under a physician's care. Midwives who attend births outside hospitals, either at home or in freestanding birth centers, are often viewed as anachronisms and treated with hostility by the medical community.

The profession itself is divided. Most midwives follow the nurse-midwifery path Kopas chose. It's generally a two-step process that starts with becoming a registered nurse, then completing a graduate-level program in midwifery.

A smaller number follow what's called the direct-entry route, which doesn't require a nursing credential. Direct-entry midwives mostly specialize in out-of-hospital birth, also called community birth. Educational options range from apprenticeships that require no college degree to graduate-level university programs.

The different routes have their own schools, professional organizations, and credentials, which have confusingly similar names: certified nurse-midwife, and, for direct-entry midwives, certified professional midwife. To add to the complexity, regulations and licensing requirements vary from state to state. Nurse-midwives can be licensed in every state, but only about two-thirds of states offer licensure for direct-entry midwives. Each state also spells out the scope of practice for midwives, which includes everything from the type of drugs they're authorized to prescribe or administer to whether they can operate independently or need physician supervision.

Those who persevere despite these challenges do so because they love the work and are committed to nurturing, hands-on care with an emphasis on childbearing. Midwives strive to develop trusting relationships with their clients and consider all aspects of their lives—physical, social, and psychological. They spend time with women. They listen to what women have to say.

Most midwives are also evangelists for their profession. They're convinced their approach—called the midwifery model of care—is better for women and babies than the standard medical model. A lot of research backs them up. In countries like Great Britain, Norway, and France, where most low-risk pregnancies are managed by midwives, maternal and infant mortality rates are far lower than in the United States, where midwives attend only about 10 percent of births. A groundbreaking study in 2018 found states with the most midwife-friendly regulations had the best outcomes for mothers and infants. Washington, New Mexico, and Oregon topped the list. States like Alabama and Mississippi, where midwives are highly restricted, had some of the worst rates of premature birth, neonatal deaths, and C-sections.

Kopas, who didn't give up her passion for research when she became a midwife, collaborated on a recent analysis of twenty thousand hospital births in Washington State that found low-risk women cared for by midwives were far less likely to have C-sections or other interventions, including drugs to induce labor or the use of forceps, than similar women cared for by obstetricians. That reduces overall costs, which makes midwifery care a bargain (important to remember when the United States has the highest rate of healthcare spending in the industrialized world). Women who give birth with midwives are also far more likely to be satisfied with the experience than those attended by obstetricians.

"There's a lot of evidence that says most women with low-risk pregnancies would be better served with midwifery care, and our healthcare system would be better served too," says Kopas.

So why is midwifery still so limited in the United States? That's a question Kopas and other activist midwives keep asking as they push for greater acceptance. It's also one of the frustrations any midwife must be prepared to deal with, says Susan Stone, president of the American College of Nurse-Midwives.

"Being a midwife is incredibly rewarding. You wake up every day feeling that you are doing something that can really improve the human condition," she says. "But don't think going into this profession that you'll just care for women and rub backs and catch babies. You may get into political situations where you have to advocate for yourself and your patients. You need to go into it with your eyes wide open, ready to fight the good fight so that you can improve the lives of the people around you."

In other words, every midwife needs to be a bit of a rebel, like the midwife in suede boots who defied the norms and offered Kopas's sister compassionate care in an era when others scorned her.

"Just being a midwife is political," Kopas says after Brumble's birth, when she finally has a few moments to rest. "You're doing something that's a little out of the norm, you're questioning the status quo—because the status quo in this country is: you get pregnant, you go to an obstetrician."

KOPAS HAS WORKED TWELVE hours, caught four babies, and her shift is only half-over. She has another twelve hours to go. As in most midwifery group practices, she and her colleagues share the load equally. They spend about three days each week in clinic, seeing patients. Once or twice a week, each midwife works a twenty-four-hour call shift at the hospital, ready to attend any patients whose birth number comes up that day.

Their home base in the hospital is an old patient room with no toilet or shower. The entryway, wide enough for one person and a chair, serves as the office. There's one computer monitor for record keeping and another that displays readouts from fetal heart monitors strapped to women experiencing prolonged or higher-risk labor. Around the corner is a single bed where the midwife on duty sleeps when she can. Lockers and stacked plastic drawers, each with a name tag, hold sweaters, socks, and bags of dried fruit and nuts. Eight pairs of sensible shoes—all black—sit in a row atop the lockers.

Kopas is at the computer again, this time to chart

Brumble's birth. During deliveries, she scrawls notes on a paper towel: time of birth; Apgar scores for the newborn; time of placenta delivery. Now she transfers that data into the system. Her next job is to check up on the four babies she helped deliver, along with two others born during the previous shift.

One came into the world via crash C-section—hospital slang for a true emergency procedure. As her mother started pushing, the baby's heart rate tanked. The midwife on duty called in an obstetrician, who tried using a vacuum device to extract the infant. When that didn't work, the only option was surgery to get the baby out as quickly as possible. The little girl hasn't been nursing well, so Kopas heads off to evaluate her first.

The midwives are responsible for their clients' babies until they're discharged from the hospital. That includes newborn exams to assess each infant's general state of health. It used to be common practice in American hospitals to snatch babies away shortly after birth to weigh, poke, and bathe them before returning them to their mothers. Nothing drives midwives crazier. "Babies are programmed to find the breast and really zero in on it right at the beginning," Kopas says. "You shouldn't be messing with that."

The period immediately after birth is sometimes called the "golden hour." It's a magical time when mother and child forge a bond that sustains them both. Skin-to-skin contact and the baby's first suckling trigger the release of hormones that cause the mother's uterus to contract, reducing the risk of bleeding. It also lowers stress in mother and baby and promotes milk production. Babies deprived of that contact can suffer anxiety and have trouble nursing.

The next baby on the list is Monique's, the first birth of the day at 8:30 a.m. Kopas finds mother and baby snuggled up together in bed, still skin to skin and exuding contentment. The baby is flushed and pink. She squalls when Kopas picks her up. The midwife lays the infant in a bassinet and runs through the standard checklist. She pinches off each nostril, to check the airways. She presses gently on birdlike clavicles, to ensure they are intact. She shines a light into eyes that are barely open. She rotates tiny hips, listening for pops or creaks.

The verdict: perfect.

Kopas chats with Monique and her husband and takes advantage of the opportunity to hold the baby a little longer and gently bounce her up and down.

"She's just beautiful," Kopas says, beaming once again.

Back in her cubbyhole, she maps out the rest of her evening. She's still got four babies and moms to check on. She'll save Brumble and her son for last, to give the family more time alone together. Then, if no more women turn up in labor, she'll be able to sleep.

Kopas doesn't really like days this hectic. It's not that she has any trouble keeping up with the workload. In fact, she seems energized when things are coming at her from all directions. But running from birth to birth means spending less time with each woman—which is not the way any midwife wants to operate.

"That's what hurts your heart," she says. "When you feel like you're not giving people enough."

3

The hospital-based midwifery Kopas practices is the latest iteration of an art as ancient as mankind. As long as babies have been born, someone has been there to catch them.

"We call it the world's oldest profession," Kopas says— and yes, she's convinced midwifery predated prostitution.

Throughout most of human history, the only help women received during childbirth came from other women—some of them skilled healers, some of them elders schooled by their own experiences. In many countries, the word for midwife is the same as the word for grandmother: *samba* in Japan, *baba* in Bulgaria, *nana* in Jamaica.

Midwives served as shamans and medicine women, concocting herbal remedies, dressing wounds, and dispensing wisdom both practical and spiritual. They were the guardians of female secrets and traditions. Childless women turned to midwives for help conceiving, while others sought ways to discreetly bring pregnancies to an end. Midwives kept the records of their communities' births and bore witness in paternity disputes. As the shepherds of new life, they were revered and respected in virtually all societies.

Early Muslim scholars described midwifery as essential to the human species, an occupation as noble as literature or music. Midwives of the Roman Empire were often enslaved women who earned their freedom through service to high-born ladies. In feudal Japan, a midwife on her way to a birth was allowed to pass through a procession of lords while other villagers prostrated themselves under penalty of death.

The rise of medicine and obstetrics didn't diminish the role of midwives in most industrialized nations. With formal training and education, midwives were integrated into the healthcare system along a natural division of labor: obstetricians attending complicated births, midwives specializing in normal. The United States is one of the few places where the medical profession forced midwifery to the margins and set out to abolish it. Obstetricians and their allies campaigned to eliminate midwives, depicting them as ignorant, filthy, and backward. The medical men insisted their only concern was for the health of women and babies, but their arguments were underpinned by racism, sexism, and economic self-interest.

Midwifery in America barely survived the onslaught. No wonder the profession still has a chip on its shoulder.

The first colonial midwives in North America were steeped in the traditions of their Old World homelands. As far back as medieval times, European midwives were women of high standing and character vetted by local authorities. They learned their trade through experience and apprenticeships. Some French villages elected midwives and paid them salaries, while local authorities granted them free passage on toll roads and ferries.

One of the first manuals for midwives, published in Germany in 1513, described the psychological aspects of the job: "Also the midwife must instruct and comfort the party, not only refreshing her with good meat and drink, but also with sweet words, giving her good hope of a speedy deliverance, encouraging and admonishing her to patience and tolerance." The book, which was used for 150 years and translated into six languages, was written by an apothecary with no expertise in childbirth—marking one of the first male incursions into what had been an exclusively female domain.

Midwives in Europe practiced their trade for centuries with little controversy until the Catholic hierarchy began to regard them with suspicion. Sickness and disability were considered punishment for sin, and midwives' ability to cure illness and pull women and babies back from the brink seemed dangerously close to powers reserved only for God. Midwives were also in a position to take life. Some clergy suspected them of killing babies and using the corpses in diabolical rituals. The *Malleus Maleficarum*—published in Germany in the 1480s and translated as "Hammer of Witches"—declared "no one does more harm to the Catholic Church than midwives."

In the four centuries of witch-hunting that followed, an estimated fifty thousand to a hundred thousand people were executed. The victims were mostly women, many of whom were burned alive. Some scholars question whether midwives were special targets, but others point out that independent, outspoken women were particularly vulnerable. "Witch-hunting was so culturally ingrained that if a midwife arrived at the scene of a birth in eastern England more quickly than expected, she ran the risk of being accused of riding her broom there," Tina Cassidy writes in *Birth: The Surprising History of How We Are Born*.

The prosecution of Barbara Lierheimer, a midwife in the German town of Nördlingin in the 1590s, is well documented. Lierheimer's troubles apparently started when she declined to attend the local executioner's wife in labor. The executioner took his revenge by spreading rumors that she was a witch. When Lierheimer complained to city officials that her business was ruined, she was arrested and tortured until she variously confessed to eating a child's foot and killing her husband after dancing with the Devil. She was tortured again and again until she died.

Historians estimate about a quarter of the women accused of witchcraft in seventeenth-century New England were healers of some sort, whether nurses, midwives, or herbalists. Boston midwife Jane Hawkins was suspected of witchcraft after attending the birth of a stillborn baby with no head. Authorities also blamed the mother, Mary Dyer, asserting the "monster" was God's retribution for her defiance of Puritan authority. Both women were expelled from the colony and Dyer was later hanged for her Quaker beliefs.

But many other midwives were esteemed members of their communities. In New Amsterdam, the Dutch-controlled territory that became New York City, midwives were municipal employees who received generous salaries and benefits. Other cities provided free housing. When Elizabeth Phillips died in Boston in 1761, her tombstone noted that in her forty years of practice she had "brought into ye world above 3,000 children."

In the American South, black and white babies alike were usually coaxed into the world by enslaved women, some of them carrying on practices and traditions from West Africa. Black babies represented income for slave owners, so capable midwives often had unusual mobility—which they took advantage of to pass messages between separated family members and help maintain community bonds. Native American and First Nations women had their own midwives and birth traditions, which few outsiders were privy to.

Historical records are dominated by women like Martha Ballard, an exceptionally hardworking midwife in Maine. Ballard began keeping a journal in 1785, when she was fifty years old. The more than ten thousand entries provide a wealth of detail about her life and work—and the obstacles she faced on a daily basis. A copy of *A Midwife's Tale*, the Pulitzer Prize–winning book based on the diaries, sits on the nightstand in the room Kopas and her colleagues share at UW Medical Center–Northwest.

In one entry, Ballard describes crossing the frozen

Kennebec River in December to reach a woman in labor. She made it most of the way before falling through the ice into an eddy. She hauled herself out, mounted a neighbor's horse, and rode to the delivery. On another day, she paddled the river by canoe in a fierce storm. On the opposite shore, she hopped from log to log to cross one stream, then waded another where the bridge was washed out. Wind uprooted a tree in her path, but her horse sprang out of the way. "Great & marvillous are thy sparing mercies, O God," she wrote. Ballard made it to her destination in time to deliver a baby girl.

Despite their heroic feats, midwives in America were already imperiled by the time Ballard died in 1812. A new breed of practitioners who called themselves men-midwives began to set up shop in American cities after receiving medical training abroad. They presented themselves as a modern alternative to the humble female midwife, better educated and better equipped, with skills and tools women did not possess.

Their models were famous men-midwives in England, like Peter Chamberlin, who invented forceps to safely extract babies stuck in the birth canal. It was a desperately needed innovation. Before that, the only solution was to call in a barber-surgeon with claws and hooks to pierce the baby's skull after it died in utero and wrench the body free. Chamberlin and his family kept their design secret for more than a century; some men-midwives dressed in women's clothes when they attended births, in order to conceal the instruments under their skirts.

As competition between traditional midwives and men-midwives intensified in America, training and education for both doctors and midwives were being strengthened across much of Europe. Alarmed by high infant mortality, King Louis XV of France commissioned a female graduate of the country's premier surgical college to instruct rural midwives. Angélique du Coudray, who called herself "Madame" though she never married, designed and built ingenious, life-sized models of women's lower torsos with birth canals that stretched and cloth babies of various sizes. In public hospitals in Paris and London, midwives and doctors honed their skills, sometimes working side by side. Midwifery training in Denmark started in the early 1700s and included instruction from a physician, apprenticeship with an experienced midwife, and a qualifying examination.

The fledgling United States government provided no public funding to educate doctors or midwives, and women paid the price. Midwives were barred from using forceps and drugs like ether because they had no formal training. Inexperienced doctors courted patients by promising more scientific deliveries, then felt obliged to use tools and medications that often did more harm than good.

Martha Ballard described one exasperating encounter with a young doctor, summoned by the husband of one of her patients. The doctor gave the laboring woman twenty drops of laudanum, a tincture of opium. The sedative put her into such a stupor that her contractions, which Ballard judged had been progressing nicely, stalled for hours. Only after the drug wore off and she vomited was the woman able to give birth to her first child, with Ballard's assistance. "I left her Cleverly at 10 & walkt home," the midwife wrote, thumbing her nose at the doctor in the privacy of her diary.

Male doctors also tried to undercut the competition by questioning women's intelligence and ability to cope with crises. "They have not the power of action, or that active power of mind, which is essential to the practice of a surgeon," said a pamphlet published in Boston in 1820. But any woman who set out to master the necessary skills would lose her standing as a lady. A prominent Boston doctor inadvertently revealed the true reason for the attacks when he wrote, "If female midwifery is again introduced among the rich and influential, it will become fashionable and it will be considered indelicate to employ a physician."

The doctor needn't have worried. Upper-class American women were increasingly persuaded to put their trust in male doctors wielding the latest equipment. By the turn of the twentieth century, physicians were attending almost half of all births. The populations still served by midwives were mostly poor and powerless—immigrants, African Americans, and rural residents.

The rise of hospitals pushed midwifery even further from the mainstream. In 1900, only 5 percent of American women gave birth in hospitals. By 1939, three-quarters of urban babies drew their first breaths in a delivery room. Women flocked to the gleaming new facilities in search of safer, less painful deliveries. But that wasn't always what they found.

As hospital births proliferated, rates of maternal and infant mortality actually increased. An analysis in New York City blamed the majority of women's deaths on doctors' carelessness, poor skills, and lack of training. Women attended by doctors had a nearly 60 percent higher risk of death than women cared for by midwives. Many physicians admitted they had never seen a birth before they started practicing and decried their own "meddlesome obstetrics"—the over-zealous use of drugs and instruments that sickened and mangled women and babies. Deadly puerperal fever, an infection spread by doctors and nurses, was also rampant in hospitals.

"Why bother with the relatively innocuous midwife when the ignorant doctor causes quite as many unnecessary deaths?" asked J. Whitridge Williams, a professor of obstetrics at Johns Hopkins. But Williams's solution, widely endorsed by his colleagues, was to elevate the training of obstetricians and do away with midwifery. Physicians mounted a vitriolic assault on the country's remaining midwives, who were overwhelmingly black and immigrant women. In the early 1920s, women and babies in America were dying at rates two to three times higher than in any other industrialized nation, and doctors found an easy scapegoat in what they called "the midwife problem."

Many of the crusading physicians wanted to improve women's health, but financial pressure and prejudice were powerful motivators for marginalizing midwives as well. Obstetricians had to earn a living, and every woman attended by a midwife was money out of their pockets. The young specialty was also desperate for training, which meant funneling poor, immigrant women to teaching hospitals.

That the midwives and pregnant women involved belonged to ethnic groups viewed as inferior only strengthened the doctors' assertions of superiority.

In pamphlets, women's magazines, and presentations to ladies' clubs, obstetricians portrayed traditional midwives as dangerous, dirty, and illiterate. Ethnic and racial slurs were common: black grannies were described as serving rat pie and practicing "African voodoism"; Italian women were superstitious; older midwives were derided as ignorant crones.

The irony is that many immigrant midwives were better trained than American doctors. Italian midwives in Philadelphia had maternal mortality rates almost ten times lower than the city's physicians. In the Massachusetts mill town of Lawrence, each successive wave of immigration brought its own midwives: German, Portuguese, Syrian, Russian, and Turkish. The city's busiest birth attendants were all literate women who had graduated from midwifery and obstetrical colleges in Europe. They also offered a good deal. In a city where the average mill worker earned $8.76 a week, doctors charged ten dollars to deliver a baby and insisted on cash. For five dollars—cash or kind—a midwife stayed throughout labor and delivery, provided daily checkups after birth, and helped cook and clean until the woman was back on her feet.

Black southern midwives, called dim-witted and a "relic of barbarism," served a population scorned by white physicians. Lay midwife Margaret Charles Smith, honored decades later with the key to her Alabama hometown, had to drive patients nearly two hundred miles to the closest hospital that would accept them. When white police officers pulled her over for speeding, she often charmed them into providing an escort. Some of the first federal funding to improve maternal and child health was earmarked to educate and license traditional midwives in Mississippi, North Carolina, Alabama, and other states—because they were the only caregivers available to most women.

In the end, none of it mattered to the fate of midwifery. The medical establishment was intent on bringing the age-old profession to an end. Training programs for lay midwives were just a stopgap measure. Maternity care in America veered sharply from the midwife's philosophy that birth is a natural part of women's lives. Instead, a medicalized view prevailed, and every birth came to be seen as a potential disaster.

Labor is "a decidedly pathologic process," wrote Dr. Joseph B. DeLee, a founding father of obstetrics who was convinced few women could escape serious damage without a doctor's assistance. In fact, he wondered if nature had intended women to die after childbirth, like salmon. DeLee's solution was an interventionist approach that included sedating every woman, making a cut in the vaginal opening, called an episiotomy, to ease the baby's passage, then extracting the child with forceps. The only setting for such a regimented approach was the hospital.

By 1950, 88 percent of American women delivered in hospitals. The few midwives who remained were mostly in impoverished communities in the South and Southwest. State after state adopted laws and regulations that either outlawed midwifery or made it nearly impossible to practice. In the world's richest country, the world's oldest profession was on the verge of extinction.

It would take a convergence of two forces to breathe new life into the craft. The first was the creation of an entirely new type of midwife. The second was a social and cultural revolution that inspired women to take the miracle of birth back into their own hands.

4

Mary Breckinridge was an unlikely savior for American midwifery.

Born in Memphis, Tennessee, in 1881, she seemed destined for the life of a southern belle. Her father was a congressman and ambassador to the court of Tsar Nicholas II of Russia. Her grandfather served as US vice president before switching allegiance to help lead the Confederacy during the Civil War.

After an elite education, Breckinridge married a lawyer. When he died two years later, she decided to become a nurse—an unusual choice for a woman of her standing. Breckinridge remarried after nursing school and gave birth to two children. Her daughter was premature and lived only a few hours. Her son died at the age of four. The tragedies were a turning point for Breckinridge, who ended her unhappy marriage and dedicated herself to children's health.

The first midwives she encountered were European

women, also trained as nurses, whom she met while help-ing French villages recover from the devastation of World War I. Breckinridge marveled at their skill and competence. She envisioned a corps of similarly trained women tending residents of impoverished rural communities in America, where healthcare was abysmal and few doctors cared to practice. Breckinridge was outraged by the vast resources devoted to war and the paltry attention paid to the deaths of women and children. "We have lost more women in child-birth in our history as a nation than men in battle," she would later argue, as she set out to establish America's first nurse-midwifery service.

Breckinridge decided to launch her experiment in the hill country of eastern Kentucky—the heart of Appalachia and one of the poorest places in the United States. Her plan was to deploy nurses with special midwifery training to visit women in their homes and care for them from the start of pregnancy through the first weeks of their babies' lives. Patterned after a service Breckinridge had studied in rural Scotland, the midwives would also teach hygiene and nutrition and offer vaccinations and other basic health care.

It was a hard sell from the start. Breckinridge's applica-tions for government funding were rejected. Medical groups were skeptical. Undeterred, Breckinridge mounted a private fund-raising blitz, trading on her family's social and political connections. Short and stout, with her hair cut shockingly short, Breckinridge was known for plainspokenness—and a tendency to curse. But she was able to charm the wealthy and influential into helping her cause. One of her biggest supporters was Clara Ford, wife of automobile tycoon Henry Ford. Eleanor Roosevelt also backed the project.

Many potential benefactors were fellow southerners, and Breckinridge tapped into the racist and anti-immigrant attitudes prevalent at the time to portray the Appalachians as the "worthy poor" by virtue of their English roots. A film Breckinridge used to promote her project was even more explicit, declaring "we pure-blooded Americans . . . are the inheritors of this wonderful country, and we are very distinct from the foreign-born element which is overpowering us in the great cities."

Whatever the donors' motivations, the appeals worked. Breckinridge launched her Frontier Nursing Service in 1925. The project eventually expanded to cover a thousand-square-mile area of isolated mountain country where women averaged nine births over their lifetimes. The per capita income was one-seventh the national average.

The first nurse-midwives to arrive in Kentucky were all educated abroad, mostly in England, where Breckinridge earned her own certification. The outsiders initially got a chilly reception. Residents were wary and local midwives resentful. Breckinridge, who ran the operation like a general, instructed her nurse-midwives to be courteous and respectful to the "grannies" who had been attending births in the region for so long. Soon, almost every woman wanted her baby delivered by the newcomers with their well-stocked bags and spotless uniforms.

To reach their patients, the midwives road horseback across mountain streams and the dizzying slopes that made the area so inaccessible. At a time when pre- and postnatal care were virtually nonexistent in the United States, the FNS midwives visited women repeatedly, before and after the birth. The fee for a complete course of maternity care was five dollars, though many families paid with eggs, butter, animal feed, and firewood. For an additional dollar a year, the midwives would tend to the healthcare needs of the whole family.

The romantic image of young women astride horses with babies tucked into their saddlebags attracted coverage in magazines like *Harper's*, *The Nation*, and *Good Housekeeping*, and helped keep donations rolling in. Even after Jeeps replaced horses, the FNS continued to attract the type of recruits who in later generations would join the Peace Corps. "FNS was one of the few places adventuresome young women could find creative, idealistic jobs," one alumna wrote. Presiding over births miles from the nearest road and doctor, the midwives also enjoyed a level of independence few other female professions could match.

The impact of Breckinridge's experiment on the people of eastern Kentucky was remarkable. Between 1925 and 1939, Breckinridge's nurse-midwives delivered three thousand babies and lost only two mothers—a mortality rate nearly ten times lower than the national average. They rarely used forceps or had to fetch a doctor for emergencies. Even though many of the patients were high-risk, the rate of complications was far lower than in the rest of the country.

Despite the excellent results and low cost, Breckinridge was stymied in her plans to expand to other parts of the country. Funding withered as the nation sank into the Great Depression, then mobilized for yet another world war. When the fighting started, British-born midwives returned home, and American women could no longer travel abroad for education. Breckinridge launched her own school in Kentucky to train nurse-midwives. But it wasn't clear that the graduates would ever find a place in American medicine.

"In many ways [nurse-midwives] stood outside the health-care establishment, challenging the notion that childbirth required male physicians, hospitals, and interventions," Laura Ettinger writes in *Nurse-midwifery: The Birth of a New American Profession*. "They also challenged the health-care hierarchy: neither fish nor fowl, nurse-midwives couldn't be easily characterized."

Breckinridge had introduced a new sort of midwife— schooled in science and more capable than many doctors. She had shown that the personalized care provided by midwives could dramatically improve the health of women and babies even under the harshest of circumstances. But like the granny midwives of the South, Breckinridge's nurse-midwives appeared to be just another dying breed.

BY THE MIDDLE OF the twentieth century, the typical American birth was an assembly-line affair. Women checked into the hospital, where they were stripped, given 3H enemas ("high, hot, and a hell of a lot"), and shaved.

Sensations were dulled with an injection of morphine followed by the amnesiac drug scopolamine. The combination was called "twilight sleep" and women demanded it. Few understood the drugs erased the memory of pain but didn't eliminate the pain itself. In their drug-induced haze, women screamed and thrashed so wildly, nurses bound them to their beds. Husbands and other family members had no idea what was going on behind closed doors because they were banned.

When birth seemed imminent nurses wheeled each woman to the delivery room, where they strapped her arms down, fastened a blindfold over her eyes and a band over her chest, locked her feet into raised stirrups and draped her body with sterile cloths. The only thing visible to the physician was her vaginal opening. Episiotomies were routine. So was the use of forceps and drugs to speed labor when doctors felt the process was taking too long. New mothers often awoke with no memory of labor and no recognition of the swaddled infants presented to them. The system was designed for the convenience of doctors, not the care of women.

"My first child was born in a Chicago suburban hospital," one woman told the *Ladies' Home Journal* in 1958.

"I wonder if the people who ran that place were actually human. My lips parched and cracked, but the nurses refused to even moisten them with a damp cloth." Another woman was strapped to the delivery table from Saturday morning to Sunday afternoon and reprimanded by a nurse for freeing a hand to wipe the sweat from her face. "If it had not been for a kind old lady who used to be a midwife in Germany, I doubt if I would have come out sane."

Some women described nurses tying their legs together to prevent birth until the doctor got back from dinner. Women of color suffered even worse treatment at the hands of white doctors and nurses who believed them to be insensitive to pain. One African American woman described a doctor comparing her to a horse and telling a nurse "now these here women you don't have any trouble with."

"The obstetric comparison between the automobile assembly line and the mother was not without relevance," Richard and Dorothy Wertz write in *Lying-In: A History of Childbirth in America*. "Birth was the processing of a machine by machines and skilled technicians." Circumventing this system was nearly impossible. The renowned anthropologist Margaret Mead had to enlist powerful men to help her obtain an unanesthetized delivery in a New York hospital. Her wish to hold and breastfeed the newborn was ignored. Nurses whisked the baby to the nursery as the rules demanded.

Meanwhile, in postwar Britain, the role of midwives was actually expanding with the introduction of the National Health Service, which provided free medical care to all. As dramatized in the BBC series *Call the Midwife*, nuns and nurses trained in obstetrics established prenatal clinics and performed home deliveries for women in teeming neighborhoods like London's East End. Hospital births soon became the norm in the United Kingdom as well, though often with midwives in attendance.

England was the birthplace of the natural childbirth movement, a term coined by obstetrician Grantly Dick-Read. His 1942 book *Birth Without Fear* became an international sensation and launched a popular revolt against mechanized childbirth. Dick-Read believed motherhood was a woman's divine purpose and railed at physicians who interfered with the experience. The sound of her baby's cry "imprints such sweet joy on her consciousness that for all time she can return to that sweet music and live again the crowning moment of her life," he wrote. Because he found it unthinkable that God would allow the act of procreation to culminate in misery, he blamed women and modern society for the pain of childbirth.

He was convinced that by fearing birth, women brought the agony down upon themselves. His approach was to break the cycle through education that reacquainted women with the natural process of pregnancy and birth, combined with exercises and deep breathing to strengthen muscles and release tension. Dick-Read preached that labor and birth should be a family affair, with husbands and wives together. Babies should stay with their mothers instead of being segregated in sterile nurseries.

Dick-Read's flair for self-promotion grated on many of his fellow obstetricians. One critic compared him to Liberace and Elvis Presley in his ability to whip up hysteria. The French obstetrician Fernand Lamaze, who popularized relaxation techniques for birth, was a bitter rival. But both men's basic ideas were later validated by science: childbirth may rarely be pain-free, but fear can make it worse by triggering the release of chemicals that slow labor; simple steps to alleviate anxiety can help.

At the time, Dick-Read was celebrated for being one of the few experts to publicly question a system that left women of all races and income levels feeling abused. Among his biggest champions were America's nurse-midwives, a few dozen women still determined to save their profession and make a difference. The superstar doctor's 1947 US tour, which included lectures at fourteen East Coast universities and medical institutions, was sponsored by the Maternity Center Association of New York. Founded in Harlem in the early 1900s to tackle the city's shocking rates of maternal and infant mortality, the MCA was an ideological sister to Breckinridge's Frontier Nursing Service. Outside Kentucky, it was the only place in the country to harbor nurse-midwives. They ran prenatal clinics and helped their mostly black and Puerto Rican clients give birth at home.

In 1931, Breckinridge dispatched one of her protégées to New York to help the MCA establish the country's first permanent school to train nurses in maternity and infant care. Her own school in Kentucky opened in 1939 and today trains more nurse-midwives than any other program in the United States. Veterans of the two schools helped found another in Tuskegee, Alabama, to train black nurse-midwives. A fourth soon followed in New Mexico.

Graduates of the new schools began to infiltrate the medical system like sleeper agents, working mainly as nurses and administrators, quietly doing their best to make things better for women and babies. Dick-Read's message meshed perfectly with the nurse-midwives' philosophy and provided an unprecedented megaphone. His public talks attracted huge crowds. And as the midwives hoped, his tour inspired some of the country's first attempts to change the American approach to birth.

At Yale University, the wives of medical students demanded natural childbirth classes and deliveries—and got them. Midwives helped plan the program and staff it. Similar projects were unrolled at other East Coast hospitals and universities, with midwives among the organizers. Midwives orchestrated some of the first programs to allow fathers to be present during birth. They demonstrated that it was safe for mothers and babies to "room in" together. In hospitals where the routine called for babies to be snatched away and bottle-fed in nurseries, they encouraged breast-feeding.

It was the postwar baby boom that first nudged significant numbers of midwives into hospital practice. With too few obstetricians to handle the country's exuberant reproduction, nurse-midwives helped fill the gap by presiding over uncomplicated births in a handful of medical centers.

Numbering fewer than three hundred nationwide in

the early 1950s, nurse-midwives were nevertheless helping birth a revolution in American maternity care. But what ultimately ensured the profession's survival was the fact that women wanted what midwives offered. Demand skyrocketed during the social and cultural upheaval of the 1960s and '70s. Feminists rejected male-dominated medicine and set out to reclaim their bodies and the process of birth. A new generation of lay midwives emerged in cities, communes, and rural communities. Working underground and outside the law, they learned from each other and emphasized the spiritual dimensions of birth. Hospitals scrambled to provide more sensitive care by adding nurse-midwives to their staffs.

In 1969, when *Redbook* magazine reported on "The Return of the Midwife," there were fewer than one thousand nurse-midwives in the United States attending less than 1 percent of births. In 2020, there are nearly thirteen thousand. Almost four hundred thousand babies a year are born into the hands of a midwife. In eight states, midwives deliver more than one in five babies born vaginally.

The expansion was hard-fought. Midwives battled state by state to gain recognition, privileges, and respect. A profession that seemed destined for oblivion was reinvented, then reinvigorated, by a tiny group of pioneers who were convinced they had something valuable to offer—and the legions of women who agreed with them.

"We continue to survive because one of the things that defines the character of a midwife is determination," says Helen Varney Burst, an early nurse-midwife and author of the first textbook on the subject. "If what you're fighting for is the woman, her baby, her family, and her ability to access the kind of care she wants—then you have to keep going."

5

The monthly meeting of the UW midwives was supposed to start an hour ago, but Kopas got sidetracked.

One of her patients gave birth in the front seat of the car on the way to the hospital. The woman's stunned husband pulled over and called 911. When the EMTs arrived, they clamped the cord and were intent on delivering the placenta when Kopas—who was on the phone with the husband—told them to head straight for the emergency room instead. The woman had had problems expelling the placenta during previous births, and the last thing Kopas wanted was for her to hemorrhage in transit. The midwife rushed to meet the ambulance.

The baby was fine. But as Kopas had feared, the placenta was stuck, and the mom was bleeding heavily. Kopas called in an obstetrician, who performed a D&C. Mom, dad, and baby were finally reunited. They were even beginning to realize that once the shock wore off, they would have a heck of a story to tell.

When Kopas belatedly joins her colleagues, she apologizes and fills them in on the details. The group is gathered around a small table in a conference room that doubles as a storage space. Metal shelves are crammed with packets of gauze pads and tubs of holiday decorations. Boxes are stacked on the floor.

These meetings are a chance for the midwives to find out what's going on in each other's lives and share hospital scuttlebutt, but the main goals are substantive. One item on today's agenda is new protocols for older mothers based on evidence that the risk of stillbirth increases sharply once they pass their due dates. Another is how best to talk to women about monitoring their babies' movements—a key indicator of vitality. Kopas scours the medical literature for the latest research, and the midwives discuss how best to integrate it into their routines.

Kopas recently attended a conference on nutrition, and she floats an idea she learned about there: asking pregnant women to keep a food diary as a way to improve eating habits. "Maybe I could make up a form and we could just offer it to people and suggest they write down what they eat once a week?" she asks.

Some of the midwives say they already discuss it. "I always talk about foundational things, like stress, hydration, food," says Victoria Swarthout, the newest member of the group. Cindy Rogers, the longest-tenured with thirty-one years' experience, cautions that diet can be a sensitive subject. "Women have a lot of issues around food," Rogers says.

There's no decision, just a conversation. Kopas doesn't issue mandates. She's technically the boss, but her leadership is collaborative, not hierarchical.

That's one of the things that makes the midwives' group more like family than coworkers, Swarthout said before the meeting. "Mary Lou made it really clear, even in my interview, that everyone in this practice is equal." Swarthout, who joined right out of school, recalled working one of those rare four-birth shifts with Kopas during her orientation. When their pagers went off simultaneously, signaling another pregnant woman was on her way, the two midwives looked at each other and broke out laughing.

"She's a very seasoned, experienced person, and I'm the brand-new person, and it really felt like we were partners doing this work together," Swarthout said. "That's something I really admire about Mary Lou."

Swarthout came to midwifery through an interest in women's health. She followed a direct route, graduating first from nursing school, then earning a master's degree in midwifery through Frontier Nursing University—the program Mary Breckinridge founded in 1939. Mary Bolles, another of Kopas's partners, helped deliver a friend's baby in a cabin in the woods when she was nineteen, then worked for years as a lay midwife in California. She decided to go to school to become licensed after another midwife in her circle was prosecuted—and acquitted—in connection with a baby's death.

The UW midwives span multiple generations. One is a former organic farmer with five children. Two have no kids. Five are white. One is part Arab. They each took different paths to the profession, though few were as circuitous as Kopas's.

The youngest of four children in a Catholic family, Kopas grew up near Worcester, Massachusetts. Her mom was a homemaker. Her dad was a dentist—a career he didn't pick for himself. His six older siblings dropped out of high school and followed their father, a Czech immigrant, into the town's fabric mills. Every week they handed their paychecks to their mother. Kopas's father was presented with two options: doctor or dentist, no dissent allowed.

He never understood Kopas's decision to become a midwife, when she could have been an obstetrician instead. "I told him those weren't my people," she recalls.

Kopas started college with only one goal in mind: to become a scientist. With loans, scholarships, and help from her dad—her parents were divorced by then—she enrolled in Colby College, a small liberal arts school in Maine founded in 1813. Kopas was an academic standout, particularly in her chosen field of biology. Her organic chemistry professor was the first to urge her to go to medical school. But Kopas was turned off by the anxious vibe from the premed crowd, who seemed more concerned with grades than anything else.

She enjoyed hiking and exploring the Maine countryside. She also assisted her ecology professor in his research on invasive species in Hawaii. Kopas's job was to sort through the stomach contents of dead rats and mice he had trapped, identify the insects they were eating, and record and analyze the data.

She was already zeroing in on environmental science when a program called SEA Semester at Woods Hole, Massachusetts, steered her toward the ocean. Half the time was spent in the classroom with lectures on marine ecology and the history of ocean exploration. The other half was learning to sail and live aboard a 125-foot, two-masted schooner.

All in their early twenties, the group met the boat in Miami and spent six weeks sailing to the Bahamas, Bermuda, and back to Woods Hole—thirteen hundred miles across the open ocean. They learned to use a sextant and navigate by the stars, work the sails, and stand watch. One of the things that stuck with Kopas was the way a community formed among the thirty-five people on board. "The idea is you're there for everyone," she says. "Our lives depended on each other." It's one of the lessons from her varied life experiences she carries over into her work as a midwife—the importance of having a community of people you can count on.

Another is the value of collaborating across disciplines. Oceanography draws from biology, chemistry, physics, geology, and ecology. Specialists work together to leverage their expertise. It's kind of like working in a hospital, where nurses, physicians, therapists—and midwives—cooperate for the benefit of their patients.

After her SEA semester, Kopas was hooked on sailing and marine science. She landed a slot on a tropical ecology field study in Anguilla in the Caribbean, where she snorkeled on coral reefs, ate two-goat stew with the locals, and studied pelicans and their fishing grounds. After graduating, the next logical step was a PhD. Kopas's undergraduate résumé earned her a slot at the University of Rhode Island, one of the country's top schools for oceanography. At first, her focus was broad. She was interested in ecosystems and how they were affected by the things humans do—like building septic systems and generating urban runoff. The group she joined was gathering data on dozens of parameters, from water chemistry to nutrient flow, as part of an ambitious effort to build computer models of coastal ecology.

Kopas was itching to go back to sea, but the project's focus was the interface between land and water. Instead of bluewater sailing, she and her fellow students buzzed around coastal inlets in a Boston Whaler motorboat collecting water samples and bits of eel grass. Kopas's dissertation topic was how nitrogen pollution from fertilizers and sewage derailed natural nutrient webs.

She loved the group's weekly seminars with their major professor, where they would pose deep, interesting questions and pick each other's brains. But she came to dread feeling hemmed in by the limited scope of her research. "In most science you have to do a deep dive into one small question," she says. "I was beginning to think I didn't want to spend my life on narrow problems."

It dawned on Kopas that she wasn't nearly as committed as the other graduate students. "I was doing great gradewise, I just felt like I was a phony and I didn't belong there." Once again, she realized "these were not my people." Basic research, which had seemed so exciting, now felt irrelevant. It was the late 1980s, an era when the ozone layer was in tatters and rich nations were using poor countries as dumping grounds for toxic waste. Climate scientists were beginning to sound the alarm about global warming. "I was seeing a lot of problems in the world," Kopas recalls. "I wanted to do something more tangible than just study ecology. I wanted to be the one making the change that would actually help communities."

She decided to take some time off from school and work for a cause she believed in. Kopas got a position at the Public Interest Research Group, a national environmental organization based in Boston. Her first assignment was canvassing door-to-door in Worcester. The Blackstone River, which passes through the former manufacturing hub, was listed by the EPA in the early 1990s as one of the country's most contaminated waterways. Kopas was helping drum up support for a toxics reduction bill, which was eventually adopted by the state legislature.

Soon she was running the canvassing operations. Kopas traveled to Boston for meetings with state legislators and lobbyists and learned what it takes to change minds and laws. She became adept at recruiting idealistic young people willing to knock on doors in unwelcoming neighborhoods. "I discovered I had some good organizational skills and that I liked working with human beings," she says. "That was part of what was missing for me in science."

It was during her time as an activist that Kopas met her future husband, an environmental attorney. They both worked at the same organization for a while. Kopas helped with administrative stuff and put her science background to work researching chemicals and tracking down expert witnesses for court cases. The pace was grueling, with eighty-hour workweeks and meager pay. Even though she still didn't know where she would land, Kopas felt she had to break away. "I needed to take the next step, whatever that was."

When Kopas talks about that period now, she describes it as a crisis. Science had been her dream for so long, she was feeling panicked about finding something to replace it. She remembered her sister's experience with a midwife. Kopas never met the woman but credits her with helping her sister and niece form a strong bond that helped get them through their first, tough years. "I think that's part of why (my niece) turned out to be a well-adjusted adult," Kopas says. "She had a pretty good start in life."

Midwifery seemed like it might tick most of the boxes on Kopas's list of what she wanted in a career: to help people in a tangible way; to do something meaningful; to stay connected to science. She went to the Boston Public Library to do some research.

The first book she checked out was *Spiritual Midwifery*. Written by Ina May Gaskin, a hippie from a commune in Tennessee, the 1976 book helped launch the modern home birth movement and inspired many of today's elder generation of midwives. Gaskin had no formal training. The first baby she delivered was in a converted school bus, part of a caravan following her guru husband on a cross-country speaking tour. After the acolytes settled into the "intentional community" they called The Farm, Gaskin expanded her midwifery services and set out to learn everything she could about birth.

Still active at the age of eighty, Gaskin might be the closest thing to a rock star the profession has ever had. She's the author of five books, a frequent speaker at research conferences, and the only midwife to have an obstetrical procedure named after her. The Gaskin maneuver is a technique to free a baby whose shoulders are stuck in the birth canal by having the mother get down on her hands and knees.

Spiritual Midwifery emphasizes both the practical and mystical aspects of helping a new human into the world. There are dozens of birth stories, illustrated with black-and-white pictures and replete with terms like "far-out" and "psychedelic." Diagrams show fetuses in every conceivable position along with techniques to extract them. Gaskin also offers guidance for midwives. "Pregnant and birthing mothers are elemental forces," she writes. "In order to understand the laws of their energy flow, you have to love and respect them for their magnificence at the same time that you study them with the accuracy of a true scientist."

With its flower-power sensibility, the book was dated even when Kopas discovered it. But she was mesmerized. "I read it cover to cover, then started checking out every book I could find on birth and midwifery. I realized this was far more interesting to me than anything I had ever delved into. What else happens in our modern lives that is so animal and miraculous?"

Kopas was thirty years old and finally knew what she wanted to do with her life.

Then she got pregnant.

6

On a brilliant fall day that belies Seattle's rainy reputation, Kopas is working one of her regular shifts at the clinic. She's booked with patients from 8 a.m. to 5 p.m.

The average length of an obstetrician visit in the United States is 9.5 minutes. Many women say they'd be lucky to get that much time with harried doctors who don't remember anything about them. With the UW midwives, the shortest appointment is twenty minutes and many run forty minutes to an hour. Midwifery is woman-centered, which means taking the time to talk with women, to answer their questions, and to understand what's going on in their lives beyond pregnancy, Kopas explains, as she checks email and organizes files before the day gets rolling.

If a heavily pregnant woman complains of a stabbing sensation in her lower abdomen, Kopas knows the most likely culprit is round ligament pain—a common irritation caused by strain on the sinews that support the uterus. But she still listens carefully as each woman describes her discomfort. "Pregnant people want to know: is this worrisome, is it dangerous, or is it just uncomfortable?" she says. "You owe it to them to take it seriously, to assess the situation and lay hands on them. That's part of my job as healer.

"Everybody knows a story about someone who had their symptoms brushed off and it turned out to be cancer or something equally bad. I don't want to be that person who brushes something off."

Kopas's office, tucked behind the clinic conference room, is not much bigger than a closet. The bulletin board above her desk is covered with birth announcements, baby pictures, and thank-you notes from grateful parents. There's also a snapshot of her with Ina May Gaskin. "I walked into a room at a conference in Tennessee and she was just sitting there, alone," Kopas says, still thrilled by the memory.

A pile of what looks like stuffed toys proves, on closer inspection, to be anatomically correct vulvas. "They're really cool," Kopas says, picking one up and spreading the labia to show how she uses them to teach women about their clitorises. Paper elephants dangle from a string in the corner.

When she's not wearing scrubs, Kopas favors colorful, flowing clothes. Today it's wide-legged linen pants, a ruffled blouse, and turquoise and silver bracelets. Her shoulder-length hair hangs in loose waves. She sits at the computer, reviewing records for the women she will see today. Orange sticky notes cover every surface like fallen leaves, yet Kopas always seems to find the right one.

Friends and colleagues describe her style of practice as a blend of compassion and scientific rigor. "She's very passionate about midwifery and offering women choices, and she's always got great ideas," says Judy Lazarus, who was one of Kopas's professors at the University of Washington. "She really pays attention to what's changing clinically and keeps up-to-date on the latest developments." Kopas serves on multiple committees to improve midwifery and women's healthcare and is past president of Washington State's American College of Nurse-Midwives affiliate. But patients are drawn to her because of her warmth and humor.

"She's just so real, and she has a boundless energy for her work," says Kopas's colleague Deborah Blue. "She's unflappable. She can talk about anything, no matter how uncomfortable or sensitive. She just puts it out there in this way that makes people feel really safe."

With a mix of clinic and hospital shifts, a group practice like the UW's enables midwives to have predictable schedules and a life outside the job. What's lost are the one-on-one relationships traditionally associated with midwifery. "Because we share patients, we have to carry this thread that we all participate in—from the beginning of someone's prenatal care through the end of their birth," says Blue. "It requires a lot of open communication, which is part of the way we work as a group." Appointments are scheduled so patients meet every midwife, but they never know who will be on duty when their labor begins.

This being midwifery, though, there are always exceptions. Women pregnant with their second, third, or fourth babies sometimes request their favorite midwife for the delivery. A woman who has experienced trauma in the past might feel more comfortable with a particular midwife. Kopas gets quite a few of those personal requests—the midwives call them "specials"—and accommodates them when she can. She's on deck at the moment for a nurse who works at the hospital and really wants Kopas to be by her side.

The clinic nurse pops her head in the office to say the first patient, Sheela, and her husband, Luther, are waiting in exam room two. The nurse lowers her voice to alert Kopas that Sheela's spirits seem low.

"Hm," says Kopas. "Thanks for pointing that out."

Kopas starts every appointment by asking the woman and her partner how they're doing and if they have any questions. Sheela, who's three weeks from her due date, says she's having a terrible time sleeping and it's affecting her mood.

Kopas listens and nods sympathetically.

"At the end of pregnancy, most people are not sleeping well," she says. "I think nature is kind of getting you ready to be up with the baby." Sheela and her husband laugh ruefully. Kopas doesn't have any magic formula to offer but suggests Sheela lie down whenever she feels drowsy, no matter what time of day. "You're getting to the point where the baby could come anytime and being rested when labor starts is really helpful because it's often an endurance thing."

It's Sheela's first pregnancy. She aspires to what midwives call physiologic birth—a more neutral term than natural birth, with no implication that births involving medical interventions are somehow unnatural. Sheela is keeping an open mind. "I think women should be able to make their own choices, whatever feels right for them," she says.

More than a third of the UW midwives' patients wind

up having an epidural when labor proves longer or more overwhelming than they expected. There's no judgment and being in the hospital makes it easy. Sheela says she likes knowing the midwives will help her cope with the discomfort, if she sticks with the drug-free plan—but will also support her if she's desperate for relief. "I've never had contractions before, so I don't have any idea what it will be like."

Midwifery care follows the arc of a woman's pregnancy. The first appointment is a chance to get to know the woman and her family, to find out about her medical history and any potential complications, and to get a sense of her personal situation—whether she has a good support network or whether she needs extra attention. Genetic testing is offered to detect rare birth defects. The highlight is the first ultrasound, which allows the parents to see their fetus and its beating heart. Monthly visits continue through the second trimester and include checkups on the baby's development and growth—and the mother's state of mind. At thirty-six weeks, Sheela is entering the home stretch, with weekly appointments until the baby is born.

She hefts herself onto the exam table, pulls up her top, tugs down the waistband of her sweatpants and lies back.

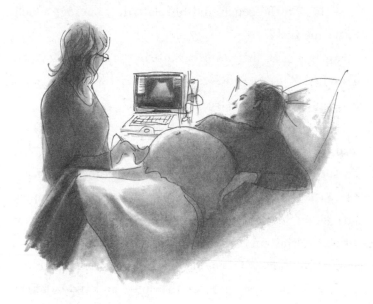

Kopas stretches a tape measure from her pubic bone, over the mountain of her belly, to the top of the uterus. The distance, called fundal height, is a way to measure the baby's growth. If all is well, the bulge should grow about one centimeter a week.

"She's moving," Kopas says, as the baby shifts under her hands. "She's saying hello."

"Oh, yeah, she's moving like crazy," says Luther. "We'll

be sitting on the couch and Sheela will be going, 'Ouch! That's my rib.'"

Kopas laughs. "It's funny because in the beginning you're all excited: 'Oh, the baby's moving!' Then by the end, you're just going 'Pipe down already, will you?'"

Kopas palpates Sheela's abdomen, identifying the baby's head, back, and shoulders by touch. It's another skill, like measuring the cervical opening, that takes time to learn. To verify the position and check the heartbeat, Kopas squirts blue gel on Sheela's stomach and traces the baby's contours with an ultrasound wand. She narrates as grainy shapes swim in and out of focus on the machine's screen. "That's the head," she says. "There's the spine and right there is the heart. See it?" She zeroes in on a small, rhythmically contracting blob.

Everything looks good. There's plenty of amniotic fluid, the baby's heart is strong, and her head is pointing down— the perfect position for birth. "The chance of her flipping over at this point is extremely low. She's doing well. She's growing fine. She's not too big. She's not too small."

Since midwives specialize in low-risk pregnancies, much of what they do is explain what's happening with a woman's body and her fetus and reassure anxious couples that everything is normal. Women with more complicated pregnancies generally aren't eligible for midwifery care. That includes women with type 1 diabetes and those who are expecting twins. Hospital midwives don't deliver babies in the bottom-first, or breech, position, but can provide prenatal care until the birth. Even in seemingly normal pregnancies complications can arise quickly. To detect potential problems, midwives have access to the same monitoring tools as obstetricians.

That includes a test to see if the mother is among the 10 to 30 percent of women who harbor group B strep bacteria in their vaginas. If the results are positive, women are treated with antibiotics to reduce the risk of infecting their baby during birth. To perform this test on Sheela, Kopas unwraps a giant Q-tip and asks Sheela to scoot down to the edge of the table and let her knees hang open.

"I'm just going to swab your vagina," she says. "Okie-dokie. All done."

As the visit winds down, Kopas asks the young couple what their plans are for birth control after the baby is born and describes some of the newest IUDs. They talk about their remodeling project and what they're doing to get ready for the new arrival. Before she leaves, Kopas recaps the couple's follow-up steps: swing by the lab for a blood test; grab naps whenever possible; expect results from the strep test in a few days. Then she's off to the next woman.

Natalie is expecting her fourth child—a surprise, but a welcome one. Kopas caught her first baby. The other two were also born with the UW group.

"I really love the midwives here," Natalie says. "They are very knowledgeable medically, but they are also caring people. There's a lot of focus on you as a mother. I've had care by OBs, and it seems to be all about the baby. Here, it's like: 'We love your baby and we'll take care of your baby—but we're taking care of you first.'"

She and Kopas laugh and joke and catch up, but the midwife has a serious mission. After one of her earlier pregnancies, Natalie spiraled into postpartum depression so extreme it verged on psychosis. She's not taking any meds now, and Kopas wants to talk about that.

Natalie says she feels good but not as cheerful as during her previous pregnancies. "I think I'm OK, and I have so much knowledge," she says. "I know what my mania looks like and how I would feel—but I'm not going to lie. It does make me nervous."

Kopas listens, her head tilted to the side. "The thing

about mania is that it's really powerful," she says in a neutral tone. "You're really productive in the early stages, which can be a good thing, so you're totally in denial."

Natalie nods in recognition but says she worries the meds might be bad for the baby.

There are risks and benefits with any medication, Kopas says. But in Natalie's case, the risk to her mental health from not being on the meds is pretty high. Perhaps she should reconnect with the psychiatrist who treated her before, and consider easing back onto mood-stabilizing drugs?

"How does that sound?" Kopas asks. Natalie agrees. "Cool, that's a plan. Now let's listen to the baby."

As Kopas deploys the Doppler, the women talk about Natalie's daughters and how her husband took the news of another kid on the way. It's too early to determine the baby's sex by ultrasound, but Natalie is convinced it will be her first boy.

Kopas ends by summing up Natalie's to-do list: get a blood draw, schedule another clinic visit in a month, and set up an appointment with the psychiatrist. To make it as easy as possible, Kopas looks up the phone number and writes it down for her.

"It's good to see you," Kopas says. "I hope it's a boy."

"Oh, it's OK," Natalie replies. "We have a girl name picked out too."

Kopas dashes back to her office to type up a summary of the visit, then moves on to exam room three.

Waiting there is Miyoko, who gave birth to her first baby six weeks ago. Here for a regular postnatal checkup, she tells Kopas she's a bit overwhelmed. "It's a good day if I get a shower." Her breasts are sore. She's starting graduate school in a few weeks and is anxious to resume working out at the gym. As the first couple in their social circle with a baby, she and her husband are having a tough time relating to friends who don't grasp how profoundly their lives have been transformed. "It's awkward because they just don't know what to make of a baby," she says.

Kopas listens and addresses Miyoko's concerns one by one. They'll do a breast exam and discuss ways to reduce the pain, she explains. She endorses Miyoko's exercise plan— "You need something outside of parenting"—and commiserates about the clueless friends. She reminds the young woman that it's only been six weeks and she's juggling a jillion things. "You're very high functioning, Miyoko."

Kopas asks if Miyoko has any trouble peeing and pooping. She also asks about birth control and explains that postpartum sex can be a little challenging at first. Hormone levels drop, so her vagina will likely be drier than usual. "You might need a little more foreplay," Kopas says. "It comes back slowly."

Certified nurse-midwives don't just deal with pregnancy and birth. Their scope of practice is wide-ranging: it extends to most of the primary care a woman needs from adolescence through menopause. CNMs can prescribe birth control, conduct physical exams, order lab tests, insert IUDs, treat urinary tract infections, and perform PAP smears and breast exams. They can also prescribe drugs. Some nurse-midwives perform abortions, but Kopas's group does not.

Her next patient is Tessa, who's here with her husband and two-year-old daughter. The couple turned to midwives in hopes of a gentler experience than their first birth, which spiraled into one intervention after another, leaving them frustrated and with no sense of control. Now Tessa fears it might happen again.

When Kopas measures her belly, the fundal height is the same as last week. That could mean the baby is not growing and is in trouble. It's the same trigger that set off the cascade of interventions when their first daughter was born. Tessa underwent what's called a growth ultrasound, a test to determine the baby's size and status. The test suggested—wrongly it turned out—that the baby was abnormally small. Tessa was given drugs to induce labor followed by an episiotomy. Her doctor used a vacuum device to extract the baby, which caused her uterus to prolapse, or droop into her vagina. In retrospect, none of it seemed necessary.

"I'm sorry," Kopas says. "I can see this is triggering a memory of 'Oh, no. Here we go again.'"

Tessa is close to tears. Kopas hands her a Kleenex, then lays out the options in a matter-of-fact way. Given Tessa's history, the most likely explanation for the unchanging fundal height is that the baby is growing normally but has shifted lower in the mom's pelvis, she explains. The worst-case scenario is that Tessa's placenta is starting to deteriorate, and the baby is suffering as a result. Kopas suggests an ordinary ultrasound to check the volume of amniotic fluid—a good indicator of the placenta's status. The results are reassuring.

"With a fluid level like this, I think the chance of having severe placental deficiency is pretty low," Kopas tells the couple. "That's just partial information, but it's enough for me to not feel like I need to strong-arm you into the growth ultrasound. Does that make sense?

"I hope I didn't stress you out too much," Kopas says. "If you go home and you start to worry, just give us a call."

Back in her office, Kopas says Tessa's previous birth experience illustrates the perils of relying on imperfect technology to detect problems with a pregnancy. Another example is the ubiquitous use of continual fetal monitoring in most maternity wards. Every woman is hooked up to the machines. Nursing stations in big hospitals look like air traffic control centers, with dozens of screens displaying the squiggles. It seems logical that keeping a close watch on babies' heartbeats will detect fetal distress early and save lives—but it doesn't always work that way. For low-risk women, studies show continuous monitoring has no statistical benefit. Mothers wind up being subject to more interventions because of false alarms.

Midwives strive to minimize technology and keep it from hijacking women's birth experiences. But they also need to know when technology is called for and how to make the experience less jarring. In Tessa's case, Kopas plans to see how she's feeling about the situation in a day or so and to emphasize that though there are no guarantees, the midwives will do everything they can to ensure the type of birth she wants.

"People are really vulnerable in pregnancy," Kopas says. "It's a scary thing. It can be traumatic. Some people literally have PTSD from bad birth experiences. How much confidence you can instill in them can really make a difference in how the process unfolds. You need to build that rapport and a relationship of trust, then no matter what happens you'll be able to deal with it together."

Kopas and her husband hadn't intended to start a family in 1993. Instead, they were gearing up for a long-distance relationship.

With her usual thoroughness, Kopas had researched nursing and midwifery schools and picked one of the best: the University of Pennsylvania. She paid the first month's rent on an apartment in Philadelphia. Her husband would stay in Boston, where his environmental law firm was based.

Then those plans crumbled.

Kopas had always wanted children. Once she realized she was pregnant, she decided to put her midwifery education on hold and start taking nursing courses in Boston after the baby was born. But she also found a way to leverage her pregnancy to learn more about her future profession. She located a birth center staffed by midwives forty-five minutes away and became a patient—and one-woman fan club.

"I just loved being near the midwives," Kopas recalls. "I

was starstruck by anyone with CNM after their name." The birth center was a little house with a relaxed atmosphere and nautical-themed décor. Kopas volunteered to help with filing and other office chores and looked for any excuse to hang around. She was particularly impressed with the head midwife. "She wasn't gushy, but she was smart and confident and knew her stuff." It was the first of Kopas's many "midwife crushes"—professional infatuations with accomplished veterans like Ina May Gaskin and her own mentors. "I would always think, 'I want to be like *her* when I grow up.'"

Kopas's personal experiences with birth were another form of education.

Her first son did not come easily into the world. With a snowstorm bearing down on the Boston area, Kopas and her husband headed for the birth center early in her labor. In retrospect, she realizes the midwives were probably rolling their eyes and thinking, "Oh honey, you've barely started." Labor was exhausting and dragged on for hours. "It was definitely harder than I expected," Kopas says. She transferred to the hospital across the street, where the midwives continued to care for her, and got an epidural. But she insisted on being able to turn it off when she wanted.

"I was a real pain-in-the-ass patient." With the threat of a C-section looming, her son was born vaginally after Kopas pushed for more than four hours.

Two years later, Kopas gave birth to her second son with no pain medication, less than an hour after she and her husband pulled up at the birth center.

"You can be a great midwife without ever giving birth," Kopas says. "I don't have to have had a C-section to help women who have a C-section. But your own experiences also inform whatever you do. I think having an epidural was a valuable experience and giving birth without one was also a great experience."

Kopas tried juggling nursing classes and childcare. She didn't like the coursework, which seemed like a throwback to an earlier era. She hated the idea of hiring someone else to look after her children. She put her nursing education on pause. "I was never going to be the wifey, the stay-at-home type," she says. "But it turned out I was happy being a mom. That was one of my careers."

Midwifery was always on her mind, though.

"Ever since I hooked on to this idea, I never really let go of it," she says. "I just put it in park for a while."

When her kids were little, she volunteered at a hospice

and worked occasional gigs as a postpartum doula, giving frazzled moms a chance to sleep while she watched their babies and cleaned their houses. It wasn't until her kids were older and Kopas and her husband moved to Seattle— his hometown—that she was able to resume her nursing education.

She finished her BSN—bachelor of science in nursing— in two years, then worked several years as a labor and delivery nurse to earn money and take a break from school. "I did not intend to be a labor nurse. It was just a step along the way, because I had kids and going right into graduate school seemed like too much of a push."

As a nurse, Kopas got a firsthand view of the standard American approach to birth. She learned a lot and admired many of the doctors she worked with. "For the most part I saw docs who were committed to patient autonomy, who treated people with respect and gave them the information they needed to make informed decisions." But she also witnessed situations that disturbed her—and made her angry. Women's wishes were often brushed aside by busy doctors and nurses. Kopas remembers one woman who wanted a vaginal birth but agreed to a C-section because her baby was in the breech position. Except it wasn't. The fetus had turned, but nobody checked to confirm its position before the surgery.

It wasn't uncommon for an obstetrician to brusquely recommend a C-section, then angrily stomp off if a woman objected. Kopas would step in, showing the parents the tracing from the heart monitor and spelling out the concerns and options in detail. "If you just explain, then go away for ten minutes and give people some time to think about it, they almost always make the right decision," she says. "They want their baby to be safe. They just don't want to be railroaded into it."

She also encountered shocking examples of disrespect.

One of the worst involved an immigrant woman who spoke no English. She was rushed to the operating room, put under anesthesia, and given a C-section with no explanation and no translation, even though the baby's heart rate had returned to normal and there was no immediate threat. "I can't imagine how traumatizing that was for her," Kopas says. "I thought at the time, 'I can't believe that just happened.'"

By the end of her stint as a labor nurse, Kopas was sick of it. It drove her crazy to have to stand by and watch doctors do things she thought were wrong. "Some of my nurse

friends would say, 'Are you sure you want all that responsibility, all that risk of being a midwife?' I said, 'Yes, please!'"
Kopas knew she could do a better job. She wanted to be the one in charge.

But during her time as a nurse, Kopas also learned she was not infallible.

"I used to think that if I ever did anything that was potentially harmful or made a stupid mistake, I would not be able to do this work anymore," she recalls. "Then I made a careless, stupid error."

Instead of a bag of saline, Kopas hooked a laboring woman up to a bag that contained Pitocin, which stimulates and intensifies contractions. The patient's contraction rate sped up dramatically. Kopas immediately turned off the IV. She explained to the patient what had happened, then went sobbing to her manager. "What got me over it was that the people around me, people I respected, were telling me, 'Yes, it was a stupid error, but you're not a stupid person. You're not a bad nurse.'"

The incident also revealed the way systemic issues can contribute to medical errors. The Pitocin bag was identical to the saline bag. Since then, the protocol has changed, and Pitocin is now delivered via a smaller bag.

Kopas had prided herself on being more meticulous than anyone else. That day she was humbled and learned she could bounce back. "It's important to understand how errors are made and to create systems that make it harder to make those errors," she says. "It still feels shitty to be the person who made the mistake."

Kopas had hoped to start a graduate program in midwifery before her fortieth birthday. By the time she finally enrolled at the UW, she was forty-five. And she wasn't the oldest person in her class. The nine students formed fast friendships and supported each other through rigorous classwork that included subjects like pharmacotherapeutics, pathophysiology, and pediatric health assessment.

Kopas stood out in her class, recalls Judy Lazarus, the professor who became a mentor. "She was outspoken. She was a leader in her cohort of students."

In addition to her classes, Kopas undertook a special study of the second phase of labor—the pushing phase—which was later published in a scientific journal. As a nurse she was appalled at many common obstetrical practices, like constantly checking a woman's cervix to see if she was fully dilated before giving her approval to push, coaching her on how to push, and stretching the perineum to make way for the baby's head. She took particular offense at doctors who would insert their fingers into a woman's vagina and tell her to try to force them out as a way to gauge the strength of their efforts.

"If I was giving birth and you told me to push out your fingers, I would tell you to get your fucking fingers out of my vagina," Kopas says heatedly. "Then they stretch the perineum to make it go faster, but all that does is give you this swollen, tender tissue that tears more easily. I don't know where this culture came from, but it's basically telling women they don't know how to give birth.

"I used to see situations where the doctor would come in and say, 'You're ten centimeters now! Let's start pushing!' And sometimes the women would burst into tears. It struck me as an insensitive way of shifting from the first to the second stage of labor. I'm not saying there aren't situations where people need help and when you should instruct people how to push, but it's not my go-to approach."

Kopas's analysis found little evidence to support many of the things doctors do. Much of medicine is like that, which is a never-ending source of frustration to Kopas and other midwives. Once a practice is enshrined as part of the "standard of care," it's very difficult to change. For decades

obstetricians assumed episiotomies prevented perineal tearing and were easier to repair. When researchers finally
looked at the evidence, they found routine cutting wors-
ened tearing in most cases and took longer to heal. Similarly, cutting the cord immediately after birth was adopted
as standard practice with no evidence it was beneficial to
baby or mother.

"Just because we've always done something a certain way
doesn't mean it's been proven to be the best."

Kopas's research project was part of the academic side of
the UW's graduate program in midwifery. The practical
experience comes in the clinical phase, when students work
alongside seasoned midwives, called preceptors, in a variety
of settings.

Kopas's first clinical post was a large hospital in Yakima,
an agricultural hub in central Washington. It was a busy
practice, with each midwife attending about thirty births a
month. Many of the clients were Latina farmworkers. One
of the most embarrassing episodes of Kopas's career occurred there, when her preceptor instructed her to check
a woman's cervix. The room was full of family members.
Kopas, trying to preserve the patient's modesty, covered the
woman's lower half with a drape and reached underneath

without looking. "It felt a little tight," she recalls, cracking up. "The patient says, 'You're in the wrong place.' It was the rectum, not the vagina." Kopas was mortified. Her preceptor couldn't stop laughing. "She told me, 'You'll never make that mistake again.'"

Another midwife in Yakima impressed upon her the importance of being vigilant after the placenta is delivered. "She said, 'Any idiot can catch a baby. You need to make sure the mother doesn't bleed to death afterward.'"

Kopas also worked a clinical rotation at a Seattle-area hospital, where her patients included women from East Africa who had undergone female circumcision. Parts of their labia and sometimes the clitoris were cut away, with the remaining tissue stitched together to leave an opening just big enough to urinate and have sex. The midwives cut through the scar tissue to open a space for the baby to pass through, then closed it up again if that's what the woman wanted.

Kopas encountered other patients she suspected were victims of domestic abuse, who would show up for appointments with black eyes and implausible stories. She followed one woman into the bathroom, the only place her husband let her go alone. Kopas offered help, but the woman denied there was any problem. Another patient, who was mentally impaired, had her baby taken into protective custody shortly after birth. Kopas held her while she cried.

Kopas's most unusual clinical experience was with a home birth midwife. It's rare for nurse-midwifery students to get experience outside of the hospital. The American College of Nurse-Midwives estimates that fewer than 3 percent of births attended by certified nurse-midwives occur at home. Kopas sought out a preceptorship with one of the few Seattle CNMs who specialized in the practice. Helping women birth in their own environments was thrilling to her. The process unfolds according to the woman's own vision, in a space where she's comfortable and family and friends are close at hand.

When she started looking for a job after graduation, Kopas's first choice was home birth, but she didn't want to start a solo business. Kopas is a natural collaborator, a gregarious person who loves to bat ideas around and learn from other people. The only jobs she could find in established home birth practices would have required her to relocate or work for half as much money as a hospital midwife. Hospitals offer reliable salaries, vacation, benefits, and malpractice insurance. Beyond the practical and economic considerations, hospitals are where most women choose to deliver their babies. Kopas knew that if she wanted to change the way women are treated and improve the health of women and babies, she would be more effective working within a system that cries out for improvement.

"I decided it's really important to bring the midwifery model to the hospital, because that's where most women are," Kopas says.

THE UNITED STATES SPENDS more per capita on healthcare than any other industrialized nation. Yet the United States is one of the few places where maternal mortality rates have been rising. It's unusual for American women to die in childbirth, but the rate is more than two times higher than in Puerto Rico and Vietnam. Maternal mortality rates for black and Native American women are higher still, exceeding those in Egypt and Kazakhstan. The rate of serious complications in pregnancy, including heart attack and hemorrhage, has more than doubled since 2000. Three out of ten women give birth via C-section, nearly twice the level recommended by the World Health Organization. And with all its high-tech neonatal care units, the United

States still has a higher infant mortality rate than any other industrialized nation.

More than half of US counties have no practicing obstetricians. By 2030 the obstetrician shortage is projected to be more than thirteen thousand. Midwives would be happy to fill the gap. The American College of Nurse-Midwives would like to see its members attend a quarter of births, which would require nearly a tripling of the workforce.

More midwives alone can't solve every maternity-related problem, but reams of evidence agree that the intensive, personalized care midwives provide can improve health. Kopas wants to be part of that.

"Mary Lou wants to have a social impact, rather than just an impact on the individual level," says Dr. Ali Lewis, an obstetrician and medical director for the UW midwifery group. The position is advisory, not supervisory. Lewis works closely with the midwives on protocols and ways to improve collaboration between midwives and OBs. The two women met when Kopas was a nurse and Lewis was a resident. "Mary Lou has really strong principles," Lewis says. "If she believes in something, she's willing to put herself out there more than most. She's going to try to do what's right."

Working in a hospital poses challenges for midwives

committed to putting women first. For example, the UW allows women to labor in tubs but not to give birth in the water. There's a concern babies could pick up infections or inhale liquid. Kopas thinks the prohibition doesn't make sense, especially since women like water birth—and can have it if they choose to deliver at home or in a freestanding birth center. She's also fighting for the midwives to be able to attend women who previously had C-sections but want to give birth vaginally. It's called VBAC—vaginal birth after C-section—and is allowed in many midwifery practices but not Kopas's.

"Sometimes it still feels like we are second-class citizens," she says.

The work makes up for the frustration—most of the time. "The thing about birth is that it's never the same thing twice. It's like the human experience. When I come to work in the morning, I never know what's going to happen. That's why it's so much fun."

Her due date was still a week away when Stephanie Kaydus arrived at her midwife's office for a final prenatal exam feeling energized and ready. When a cervical check revealed she was partially dilated and likely to give birth before the day was through, it seemed fitting. A perfect orb would rise in the sky that night—all her other children had been born when the moon was full. Kaydus headed home to wait.

Her midwife, Ann Olsen, began loading her SUV with enough medical equipment to stock a small clinic: oxygen tanks and masks, stethoscope, IV bags and a bass-tournament-sized tackle box brimming with needles, sutures, and vials of drugs. Olsen drove from her home in the foothills of Mount Rainier to the eighteen-acre spread south of Seattle where Kaydus and her partner, Sean Tuley, live with Kaydus's three daughters, two dogs, and a half dozen or so horses.

Olsen is a home birth midwife in the classic tradition. She's not a nurse. She didn't earn a graduate degree like Kopas and other certified nurse-midwives. She came into midwifery through the direct-entry route. But that doesn't mean she lacks education. "That's probably the biggest misconception people have about home birth midwives,"

Olsen says. "They think we have no training." Even some of her clients are surprised to hear she completed the same college prerequisites as medical students, followed by a three-year program at an accredited midwifery school. She passed national and state exams and holds designations as both a licensed midwife and certified professional midwife.

This will be the fourth baby Olsen has helped Kaydus deliver. The first was born on a New Year's morning in an independent birth center where Olsen used to practice. The other two were born at home. Kaydus also gave birth in a hospital once, with Olsen by her side for support. That baby was diagnosed before birth with a rare genetic defect and lived just a couple of months. The painful experience reinforced Kaydus's distaste for medical settings.

"I would never give birth in a hospital again," she said, during a regular checkup with Olsen two months earlier. "You feel like you're just a number on a board. It's chaotic. I believe the human body is enough; we were made for this. In a hospital they give you the feeling you need their help. You can't just relax and do what you need to like I can with Ann."

With her broad smile and motherly manner, Olsen

doesn't seem like a revolutionary. She keeps bees and passes out jars of honey to friends and clients. Her yard is a riot of flowers. But her job places her squarely at odds with medical norms—even more so than most nurse-midwives. Home birth might have been the de facto form of delivery for most of human history, but it has now become the most controversial—at least in the United States.

The subject is the third rail of online forums about pregnancy and birth. Any mention and the discussion explodes into name-calling and accusations. Opponents insist home birth is so reckless as to verge on child abuse. Proponents describe a transcendent experience that strengthens the bond between mother and child in the way nature intended and avoids the risks and pitfalls of hospital births. Dueling studies conclude home birth imperils babies—or not. Each camp attacks the other's statistics. The British Royal College of Obstetricians and Gynaecologists embraces home birth. The American College of Obstetricians and Gynecologists concedes women should be able to deliver where they feel most comfortable but follows up with a string of warnings for those who choose home.

Since doctors and hospitals began to gain dominance in the early 1900s, giving birth at home has been portrayed as dangerous and destined for extinction. Governments might not presume to tell women where they can and can't give birth, but some state regulations are so onerous or ambiguous that home birth midwives risk operating without licensure or legal protections. Against the odds, the practice has survived—and is gaining in popularity—because many families feel passionately about it.

More than thirty-eight thousand babies were born at home in the United States in 2017. That's almost 1 percent of total US births, up 80 percent since 2004. The rate is more than twice as high in states like Montana, Vermont, Florida, Oregon, and Washington with laws that support midwifery. In Nebraska, where midwives can be jailed for attending home births, only three babies out of a thousand are born at home. Certified nurse-midwives attend about a quarter of home births, but the practice is largely the domain of direct-entry midwives like Olsen.

Sometimes called lay or community midwifery, the direct-entry branch of the profession follows in the footsteps of the country's colonial, black, and immigrant midwives. A new wave of interest sprang out of the feminist uprising of the 1960s and '70s, as women challenged the establishment and asserted their rights to control their own bodies—particularly during pregnancy and birth. Since traditional midwifery had been virtually extinguished, women banded together to learn from each other and from textbooks. These self-taught midwives celebrated the power and beauty of natural birth and rejected the medicalized view of pregnancy as pathology. They held themselves apart from nurse-midwives, whom they saw as being co-opted by the system. In turn, the American College of Nurse-Midwives took a swipe at home birth midwives in the mid-1970s, declaring "the hospital or maternity home" the safest settings for delivery. The group soon reversed itself and endorsed home birth, but the rift between the two branches persists. *Med-wife* is an insult community midwives use to describe nurse-midwives so wedded to technology they might as well be obstetricians. Hospital midwives have their own term for irresponsible home birth practitioners: *cowboys.*

WHEN OLSEN ARRIVES AT Kaydus's home, the atmosphere could hardly be less hospital-like. As tall and willowy as a supermodel, Kaydus, twenty-eight, is in the kitchen making smoothies. She's wearing slippers and a black sundress with spaghetti straps. Her mother and a couple of friends are conversing around a dining room table piled with baby shower gifts. Tuley, a veterinarian, is wandering around outside, trying to stay busy. Kaydus's daughters, aged five to eight, ricochet from room to room, bored and excited at the same time. They know the new baby is a girl too.

Olsen is dressed in a tee shirt and jeans. She doesn't hover but keeps an eye on her pregnant patient, who straddles a big blue ball when contractions make it hard to stand. Kaydus and Olsen's daughter have been best friends since childhood, hanging out together at the midwife's house. Olsen was the adult the neighborhood kids came to with questions about sex, birth control, or STDs, because they knew she would give straight answers and wouldn't tell their parents. Kaydus remembers wondering if she would ever have children when she grew up—and if so, whether Olsen would deliver them. "She's like a second mother to me," Kaydus says. "I trust her entirely."

Kaydus is one of those lucky people for whom the first stage of labor—the most painful part for many women—is little more than an irritation. When a contraction strikes, she barely seems to notice. "There's one," she says casually, as if remarking on a plane passing overhead. When the spasm passes, she stretches and twists on the ball.

Olsen knows from Kaydus's previous births that her outward demeanor is not a good gauge of how things are progressing. "Everybody labors differently," Olsen says. "With Stephanie, you can't even tell it's happening." An inflatable blue birthing tub is already set up in the master bedroom and filled with warm water, and Olsen urges her patient in that direction.

The room is large, with a sliding glass door that looks out on horse paddocks, and a stone fireplace that covers most of one wall. Kaydus slips off her panties and eases into the tub, dress and all. Over the next hour, friends and family drift in and out of the room as if at a party. Kaydus's oldest daughter brings her a cookie and offers to make coffee. Tuley sits by the tub, his hands on her shoulders. Kaydus's mother reads aloud from a description of the unborn baby's astrological sign. "Libras are best known for their love of balance." Violin music plays in the background.

Kaydus and Tuley haven't lived here long, so Olsen visited a few weeks ago as she always does with new clients or new houses, to make sure the setting is suitable. Among her nonnegotiable criteria are an easily accessible bathroom for the mother and a clear path for EMTs in case of emergency. The house can't be filthy, either. A couple of times Olsen has diplomatically referred clients to birth centers if she felt their homes were too dirty, cramped, or chaotic.

There's plenty of room at Kaydus's house, and Olsen has her gear in easy reach. Home birth midwives carry much of the same equipment hospital midwives and obstetricians use during labor. They don't have continuous fetal monitors, but they do have Dopplers. Olsen checks the baby's heart rate every fifteen or twenty minutes, reaching into the tub to press the instrument to Kaydus's belly.

Olsen can monitor women's blood pressure, which is essential for detecting the spikes that can signal a dangerous condition called preeclampsia, and require a hospital transfer. She's got a pair of episiotomy scissors she's only used once. Nonnurse midwives can't prescribe medications, but in Washington and many other states, they can administer a wide range of potentially life-saving drugs. Olsen's tackle box holds four antihemorrhagic medications. She can hook women up to IVs if they need fluid and dose them with antibiotics. Olsen carries a collection kit for parents who want to bank stem cell–rich cord blood as a hedge against future disease. For babies who have trouble breathing, Olsen deploys an infant-sized, hand-pumped respirator to inflate tiny lungs. She teaches the technique to midwives in developing countries when she travels abroad for mission work.

Olsen can also stitch up vaginal tears and numb the tissue with lidocaine. What she can't offer is an epidural or narcotics. Her most powerful pain-control technology is nitrous oxide gas. But women who want home birth know what to expect and are committed to letting the process unfold as organically as possible. Rarely does one of Olsen's clients decide to pull the plug and head to a hospital just for pain relief.

Kaydus refused pain medication even when she gave birth in the hospital. Now she's beginning to shift uncomfortably as her contractions sharpen. Olsen checks her cervix and reports that she's dilating well. Otherwise, the midwife waits and watches and offers reassurance.

"Ooooh, that was a mean one," Kaydus says, letting her breath out with a whoosh as a stabbing pain begins to subside. "It felt like there was a hook that went in below my belly button and pulled down."

Olsen scoots closer to the tub.

"Take a big breath, all the way down to your toes, and shake it off," she urges, then repeats the mantra she offers every laboring woman: "A contraction lasts one minute. You can do anything for one minute. Then you get a break."

OLSEN HAS BEEN DOING this for nearly twenty years. That's not counting the first baby she caught, when she was fifteen.

A local doctor phoned one night and asked her to come over because his wife was in labor. Olsen assumed she would babysit while the couple went to the hospital. Instead, the man positioned the startled teen by the bed and supported her hands to receive the newborn. "He told me: "Don't be afraid. You're going to be doing this for the rest of your life," Olsen says.

She still doesn't know what the doctor sensed about her. They didn't discuss it at the time, and when she tried to reconnect years later, he had passed away.

"That was 1975 in southern Nevada," she said. "There were no midwives. *Nobody* had babies at home."

Olsen spent her early years on a ranch in Southern California. Her father was a Hollywood stuntman in movies and TV shows like *The Wild Bunch*, *The Big Valley*, and *The Six Million Dollar Man*. She learned to speak Spanish before English, thanks to the women who took care of her on movie sets in Mexico. Olson's mother took her own life at the age of twenty-four, stricken with postpartum depression after the birth of a younger sister. Consequently, Olsen has always been especially alert for any hints of malaise in her own patients.

Olsen spent years raising kids and helping with her husband's construction business before she was able to pursue the dream of midwifery planted by the prescient doctor. She even considered joining the Navy Reserve to get midwifery training but couldn't reconcile boot camp and military service with her responsibilities at home. Olsen was thirty-nine by the time she enrolled at Seattle Midwifery School.

Founded in 1978 by four lay midwives, the school was one of the first of its kind in the country. Obstetricians, CNMs, and midwives from other countries were enlisted to teach. Classes met on the third floor of the El Centro de la Raza building, a ramshackle school abandoned by the city, then seized and occupied by Latino activists in the early 1970s. "It was freezing cold in the winter and sweltering in the summer," Olsen said. Homeless people camped in the parking lot. Students studied physiology, microbiology, and anatomy in the classroom and gained practical skills attending births with experienced midwives. The school was accredited by the state and graduates were among the earliest lay midwives in the country to gain licensure.

Most people who want to become direct-entry midwives today enroll in one of several similar, accredited educational programs. Among them is the current version of the Seattle Midwifery School, which merged with Bastyr University, a naturopathic institution north of Seattle. Some states still allow apprenticeships instead of formal education, but that's increasingly rare.

Direct-entry programs differ from nurse-midwifery mainly in the amount of time devoted to research, policy, and broader nursing practice. While nurse-midwives can provide a wide range of primary healthcare, direct-entry midwives focus exclusively on the care of women and newborns during pregnancy and shortly after birth. Nurse-midwives can graduate without ever attending a birth outside a hospital. For direct-entry midwives, out-of-hospital birth is the main focus.

(There's also a direct-entry designation called certified midwife, which doesn't require a nursing credential but is otherwise identical in education to a certified nurse-midwife, including the requirement for a graduate degree. In 2020 the CM credential was recognized in six states.)

Every state regulates midwives differently. As of 2020, certified professional midwives could be licensed in thirty-three states. The National Association of Certified Professional Midwives, which is fighting to extend licensure to all states, estimates there are about three thousand CPMs working in the United States.

As a solo practitioner, Olsen is part of a rare breed.

She attends about forty to fifty births a year, which means most days there's a chance her phone could ring with a woman in labor at the other end. "I'm generally on call twenty-four/seven," she says. When she and her husband go out to dinner or a gathering, she drives separately. Family vacations are scheduled a year in advance. Olsen and other local midwives cover for each other in emergencies—like two babies deciding to be born on the same afternoon.

Olsen is a one-woman shop, which means she does all her own scheduling, orders supplies, negotiates contracts with insurers, and is responsible for her own malpractice coverage—which can be a major hurdle. It's easier in Washington, where companies that sell malpractice insurance must also collectively offer it to midwives. Washington is also one of several states where home birth is covered by most private insurance and Medicaid, the federal insurance program for low-income people that pays for nearly half of all US births. In states where coverage is not as inclusive, community midwives can be hard-pressed to make a living unless they serve clients who can pay out of their own pockets.

Private insurance pays Olsen about $3,200 for each woman's maternity care, which includes prenatal visits, the birth, and a month or more of postnatal care for mom and baby. Medicaid pays $2,300. Olsen estimates she clears about $60,000 a year—roughly half the average salary for a hospital-based nurse-midwife.

She considers it a good trade-off for being independent and not having to deal with hospital politics. Olsen lives in a rural community fifty miles and a world away from Seattle, surrounded by farms and forests. She works out of her house, a suburban split-level with a small sign by the door that reads "Midwifery Office." The exam room is a downstairs bedroom. Her French provincial desk and hutch dominate one wall. Women sit on a twin bed with a quilted coverlet and flowered throw pillows, instead of on a metal exam table. Bins of toys fill one corner, to occupy youngsters who accompany their moms. There's a chair for dads too. Pictures of mothers and babies hang on the walls. "The Angels Danced the Day You Were Born," says one.

Olsen blocks off an hour for each appointment and will talk about anything the woman and her family want. During one visit, she pulled out a set of life-sized fetus dolls and patiently explained the baby's positioning and growth for a seven-year-old boy who was excited about his future sibling but anxious about his mother's safety. For another couple with a due date just days away, she ran through a detailed account of what to expect, from the way she planned to lift the baby onto the mom's chest to when and how she would conduct the postnatal exam. "If you think you're in labor, call me. Don't text. Even if it's two in the morning," she said. She passed the dad a list of instructions in case the baby was too impatient to wait for the midwife. "I love seeing the husbands' faces when I give them this," she said, laughing.

Olsen makes a point of engaging women's partners and preparing them for an active role in the birth. "My goal is that the partner is the one supporting her," she explained between appointments. "At the end of the day I'm leaving, and I want the partner to be the hero, not me."

In her cozy bedroom space, Olsen runs through the same prenatal rituals Kopas and her colleagues perform in their clinic: she checks blood pressure, measures fundal height, draws blood, feels the baby's position, does vaginal swabs, listens to the baby's heart. Few home midwives have ultrasound machines, but Olsen invested in one and traveled to Texas to learn how to use it. She also sends all her patients to a specialist midway through their pregnancies for a more sophisticated scan that can spot many birth defects and other problems. A research junkie like Kopas, she helped convince the state to require a new type of cardiac screen for newborns that improves detection of heart defects.

IF THERE'S ANY CONSENSUS to be found in the dueling studies on home birth, it's that outcomes for babies and mothers are best in places where midwives are well trained and the practice isn't forced into the shadows. In the United States, where education requirements and licensure for direct-entry midwives vary by state, most studies show that while still very low, the risk of death for babies born at home is higher than for babies born in a hospital. In Canada and parts of Europe where home birth is more common and midwifery education is standardized, studies show no difference in neonatal mortality between planned home births and planned hospital births. There's no debate about the benefits to women of giving birth at home, which include much higher rates of vaginal delivery and far fewer interventions.

Cochrane, an independent network of health researchers, concluded planned home birth is just as safe as planned hospital birth, provided midwives are experienced and have collaborative medical backup for emergencies. The ease of hospital transfers was one of several criteria in a 2018 analysis that found states where midwifery is well integrated into the healthcare system have better outcomes for mothers and babies.

Women who choose home birth never want to wind up in a hospital, but sometimes it's necessary. Olsen transfers about 5 percent of her patients, far lower than the national average of 12 percent. The most common reason is an unusually long labor that isn't progressing. Rarer situations involve fetal distress, postpartum hemorrhage, or a newborn struggling to breathe. One of Olsen's worst emergencies was a woman whose uterus partly inverted like a balloon after the placenta came out.

Olsen's clients sign a contract agreeing not to resist if she says it's time to give up on home birth. "I'm an expert in what normal looks like," she says. "When it's not normal, I know what that looks like too—and when that happens, we want to be in the hospital." As she tells her clients, C-sections save lives.

Olsen has cultivated mutually respectful relationships with hospitals, doctors, nurses, and EMTs. Several local medical professionals or their spouses have turned to her to help them give birth at home. They know she takes a conservative approach and isn't going to show up at the ER with what's gruesomely referred to as a train wreck—a woman or baby in desperate trouble.

On the flip side, many home midwives have stories of being yelled at and accused of negligence by doctors and nurses during transfers, and of seeing their patients treated disrespectfully. CPMs don't have hospital privileges, so a transfer means losing control of their patient's care. Olsen stays with every woman, acting as an advocate and helping make the process as stress-free as possible. She also participates in a peer review network with other midwives and doctors, reviewing difficult cases. The group invites all new doctors in the area to join the meetings, meet midwives—and rethink their assumptions.

"Even a lot of doctors have no idea what we do as home birth midwives," Olsen says.

Olsen has never lost a woman during delivery, but she did lose a baby several years ago at the birth center. The head emerged, but the body refused to follow. Olsen figured it was shoulder dystocia, an unpredictable and frightening emergency that occurs when the baby's shoulder gets stuck behind the mother's pubic bone. It can be life-threatening if the umbilical cord is compressed. Olsen tried every maneuver she knew, including having the mother flex her knees tight against her chest, then get down on all fours. Nothing worked.

EMTs transported the mother to the hospital, but the baby was dead. A C-section revealed the cause: The child's abdomen was swollen to the size of a basketball due to a rare kidney defect that hadn't been detected during pregnancy. The little girl wouldn't have been able to live, and her parents didn't fault Olsen. But the midwife will never shake the memory. "I still have a little post-traumatic stress over the whole situation, not being able to get a baby out," she says. "And I'm really good at getting stuck babies out."

Olsen screens her patients for factors that would make

home birth too risky, like breech presentations, twins, high blood pressure, problems with the placenta, or general poor health. She won't accept women with previous C-sections or anyone she suspects of drug abuse. Olsen turns away about a third of potential clients, simply because her schedule is full.

Some women choose home birth because of traumatic experiences with doctors, hospitals, or sexual abuse. Many shudder at the idea of giving birth in a hospital full of germs and strangers. Others don't want any obstacles to physiologic birth. "I was in labor for forty hours with my first son," said one repeat client. "I know that if we had gone to the hospital I would have been screaming, 'Get me drugs!' But I just pushed through it and now I feel like Superwoman."

All of Olsen's clients love knowing that the person who cares for them throughout their pregnancies is the one who will help them deliver their babies. Olsen also thrives on those close relationships. "In my practice, I get this lovely, self-selected population that wants what I offer," she says. "They're fairly healthy, they want a home birth, they want their babies, and they're motivated to change their diets or change their behavior if they need to." She's helped one client give birth eight times and has several others who have delivered five or six babies under her guidance. A few, like Kaydus, she's known most of their lives.

KAYDUS AND OLSEN HAVE been through this tango together three times before, and they fall into a familiar pace. Kaydus is a stoic laborer, rarely crying out. This is Tuley's first child, so he doesn't realize how extraordinary that is. Kaydus schools him. "Do you know how many women would be screaming right now?" she says. But she is getting impatient. She and Olsen discuss rupturing her bag of water—the amniotic sac—which worked during her previous labors to speed the birth.

Kaydus says that's what she wants. But as Olsen gets ready, the laboring woman gets nervous. She knows once the bag is broken, the baby will come in a rush.

"I'm scared," she says.

"What are you scared of?" Olsen asks, gently. "Tell me."

"Of the pain of her coming out."

"You're doing amazing," Olsen replies. She slips a sheath called an Amnicot over her index finger. There's a toothlike hook on the end, made especially for the task. "This won't hurt at all," she says, reaching through the water into Kaydus's vagina.

Kaydus is on her knees, resting her torso on the edge of the tub as if at a swimming pool. Tuley cradles her arms.

With her bag broken, Kaydus starts pushing, breathing as heavily as a mountain climber and finally showing a few flashes of discomfort. She asks for more hot water in the tub. The music is getting on her nerves, and she implores someone—anyone—to switch it off.

"Unuhhhh," she moans. "I'm not getting a break. Ohhhh. Why did I sign up for this?"

Olsen holds a washcloth to the back of her neck. The midwife reaches into the water with the Doppler, and once again the room is filled with the steady heartbeat of a new life.

"Just focus on your breathing," Olsen says. "One, two, three. Let it out. One, two, three. Let it out."

Kaydus utters a cry that's a cross between a groan and a scream. "Here she comes!" she says.

Olsen leans over the tub and plunges both arms into the water up to her shoulders.

"Head's out," she says. "Beautiful. Beautiful."

Kaydus gasps and pushes again. A blurry form materializes

in the water followed by a blossoming plume of red. "She's here," Olsen says, scooping up the newborn and placing her on her mother's chest. "Oh, you did such a good job!" she says to Kaydus.

The baby fills her lungs and wails.

At the sound of the cries, Kaydus's other daughters—banished for the birth itself—rush back into the room. They surround their mother and exclaim over their new sister. Kaydus's tearful mother kisses her daughter on the head.

Time of birth, 7:52 p.m., with the moon shining through scattered clouds. Olsen will be here until well after midnight.

She gives the new mom a shot of Pitocin to prevent bleeding and uses a tiny bulb to suction mucus from the baby's nose and mouth. She checks Kaydus's pulse and listens to the baby's chest with a stethoscope. Kaydus cuts the cord herself. Her perineum didn't tear, so there's no need for stitching. After the initial celebration, Olsen shoos everyone out so she can deliver the placenta and help Kaydus out of the tub. When the doors are flung open again, Kaydus and Tuley are tucked into bed together. Their daughter is already nursing. Someone pops a bottle of champagne and

hands glasses around. Portuguese stew and pasta are dished up for the new parents.

Olsen types up records on her laptop and periodically checks mom and baby. About an hour after the birth, the midwife gathers the kids in the bathroom to show them the placenta and explain how it works.

"It's gross," says the five-year-old. "I don't want to touch it."

"You don't have to," Olsen reassures her.

After the youngsters have washed their hands, she lets them help with the newborn exam. They stick out fingers and squeal with delight when the baby grabs hold. Olsen seems energized, not tired. She will come back the next day, and the day after that to check on mom and baby. She also makes house calls to help with breastfeeding. While nurse-midwives often relinquish care of newborns once they leave the hospital, home birth midwives in Washington serve as primary care providers for the first two weeks of life. Kaydus will bring her new daughter to Olsen's office in about a week for her first medical appointment.

About two hours after the birth, Olsen tells Kaydus it's time to see if she can pee. "How do you feel?" Olsen asks. "I'm going to get you up to the bathroom."

As the midwife leans over the bed, Kaydus grabs her around the neck and hugs tightly. "You did such a beautiful job," she whispers.

"You did all the work," Olsen replies. "I just got to catch."

9

The Victorian mansion seemed to beckon to Laura Erickson.

The midwife was riding her bike in Portland, Oregon, and noticed a "For Lease" sign out front. The three-story house had seen hard times since the turn of the twentieth century when it was built. But the bones were sturdy, the scrolled woodwork and leaded glass windows intact.

"Midwives can be a little witchy," Erickson says. "I sat on the front step and looked up and asked, 'Is this my birth center?' I just got tingles, and a strong feeling: 'Indeed, it is.'"

That was 2004. Erickson and her contractor husband spent nearly a year ripping out shabby carpets and false ceilings, upgrading electrical systems, and refinishing floors fashioned from old-growth fir. Erickson applied her passion for design, furnishing four spacious suites with period lamps, overstuffed chairs, and beds big enough for an entire family. "The rooms have to feel very private, very homey," Erickson says. The Alma Midwifery Birth Center welcomed its first newborn in early 2005.

Along with hospitals, clinics, and private homes, freestanding birth centers like Erickson's round out the list of locations where midwives help women deliver their babies. In 2017 about twenty thousand babies were born in birth centers, almost double the number in the previous decade. Birth center midwives say the facilities offer the best of both worlds. Women can labor and birth with their families in a relaxed, homelike setting, secure in the knowledge that the center has emergency procedures in place and an established relationship with nearby hospitals. Some midwives describe it as home birth—but at the midwife's house.

"People choose us because we don't feel like a hospital," Erickson says. "The whole idea is to allow women to feel comfortable, and when they feel comfortable . . . that helps them have their babies more easily." The length of stay varies, with some facilities discharging women four to six hours after birth, and others allowing them to linger twenty-four hours or longer.

Most of the 375 or so birth centers in the United States are owned by midwives. All of them are run by midwives, in keeping with the profession's commitment to personalized care. That's not surprising, because birth centers were invented by midwives.

The first in the country was La Casita, a small adobe structure near Santa Fe opened in 1946 by the Catholic Maternity Institute. The midwives were nuns and laywomen who mostly attended home births, like Mary Breckinridge's Frontier Nursing Service. La Casita was built for families who lived too far away for convenient visits. Women loved it—too much, it turned out.

A stay of a few days at La Casita was like a mini vacation for mothers with big families. The facility had running water and electricity, which few of New Mexico's rural Hispanic residents enjoyed at home. Soon more than half of the institute's births occurred there. But delivery at La Casita was more expensive than home birth, and the clients could only afford to cover a fraction of the cost. The financial losses contributed to Catholic Maternity Institute's closure in 1969—and foreshadowed the economic challenges birth centers still face.

The modern birth center movement began in 1975 when the Maternity Center Association opened its Childbearing Center in New York City. Housed in an elegant, six-story town house near Central Park, the facility was designed to demonstrate the viability of freestanding birth centers and to establish national standards. The target clientele were women "dissatisfied with the impersonal, dehumanizing, and costly medical care characteristic of hospitals," the *New York Times* reported when the facility opened. A few months later, the newspaper chronicled one of the first births, marveling that mother and father were able to stay together throughout labor, then hop into a cab with their new baby and be back in their apartment ten hours later.

Through no fault of its own, rising malpractice insurance rates forced the center to close in 2003, but the concept caught on despite early skepticism from medical organizations. Hospitals appropriated the term and began rebranding their maternity wards as birth centers. "It's infuriating, because it's confusing to the public," says Kate Bauer, executive director of the American Association of Birth Centers. "Putting up pretty wallpaper and adding a recliner to a room is not the same as a real birth center. The model of care in a birth center is not just about the facility. It begins with your first prenatal visit. It's about being a partner in your healthcare."

A landmark study first published in 1989 and repeated

twenty years later found birth centers to be just as safe as hospitals for women and babies—with lower costs and higher satisfaction ratings. More evidence came from the five-year, federally funded Strong Start initiative, which followed forty-six thousand Medicaid beneficiaries through pregnancy and birth. Women who got prenatal care at accredited birth centers were less likely to give birth prematurely, have underweight babies, or have C-sections, even if they delivered at a hospital. Their babies were healthier too, with fewer hospitalizations and emergency room visits—and an average savings to the system of about two thousand dollars per birth.

The basic approach to midwifery care is the same whether it occurs in Mary Lou Kopas's hospital-linked clinic, Ann Olsen's home office, or a birth center. What's different at Alma Midwifery is the atmosphere.

The house feels like a luxurious bed-and-breakfast. Each birthing suite has its own bathroom and a large tub where women can labor—and give birth. Warm water is sometimes called the midwife's epidural, a natural alternative to help women relax and dial down the chatter in their minds. The Fern Room, with a fireplace and iron bedstead, features a tub surrounded by a lush, woodland mosaic. The Trillium

Room's tub is triangular, and a hand-painted henna border wraps around the ceiling with repeating, ten-centimeter circles: the diameter of a fully dilated cervix.

Even the stairway, with its ornate banister, is sometimes pressed into service by laboring women who use it to leverage themselves through squats. "We've had a baby born here," Erickson says, pausing on the landing during a tour of the facility. Inside a closet is an emergency sled to lower a woman down the stairs. They've used it once in fifteen years, Erickson says. There's a living room, parlor, and farmhouse-sized kitchen downstairs, where family members can gather and snack and wait. After a birth, Erickson's staff serves the family a meal in their suite.

Erickson and the two other midwives she employs also offer home births, but delivering babies at the birth center is more predictable for them. They know exactly where to lay out their gear and find supplies. When labors run long, they can nap or take a shower. Birth centers generally have access to the same equipment and medications as home birth midwives, depending on local regulations. Some birth centers have nitrous oxide for pain relief, but none offer narcotics or epidurals. Aside from location, the main distinction between home birth and birth center birth is proximity to hospitals and the collaborative relationships birth centers forge with local medical personnel. Birth center midwives know how long it takes to get to the closest hospital and they also know the doctors and nurses they are likely to encounter when a patient is transferred.

Erickson is a certified professional midwife who got her start in home births. She trained in Texas, where she delivered babies in buses and teepees and worked at a busy border clinic with up to six births a day. She opened her own practice after moving with her family to a farm in Minnesota, where many of her clients were Mennonite women, who shun hospitals.

Birth center midwives are about evenly split between certified professional midwives and certified nurse-midwives. Many facilities employ both. Erickson's staff used to be exclusively CPMs, but her new hires are now CNMs. Not only are certified nurse-midwives able to treat a wider range of health concerns, they are also more likely to be covered by insurance. CNMs with hospital privileges can also continue to care for women who have to be transferred because of complications.

The number of birth centers has more than doubled since 2004, but distribution is spotty. Most states regulate licensure, and nationwide only about a third of birth centers are accredited. Texas, where rules are liberal, has nearly ninety facilities. California has about fifty. New York, the fourth most populous state and the place where the modern birth center originated, had only three by early 2020 after several closures. One of the reasons was a state law, since overturned, that birth centers must be supervised by physicians. New rules allow midwives in New York to own and operate birth centers.

Running a birth center is expensive, and the key to survival is insurance reimbursement. "If you don't get paid a sustainable rate, you're going to be out of business," says Bauer. Some centers rely on out-of-pocket payments, but that narrows the client base. Private insurance companies are largely free to set their own policies, so birth center owners spend a lot of time negotiating coverage and fees. Medicaid covers prenatal care and birth at birth centers, but different states administer the program differently. Even Oregon, known for its support of midwifery, contracts with only certain birth centers. Alma Midwifery is not on the list, but one of Erickson's newest competitors is.

Less than five miles away, the Midwifery Birth Center is owned by Women's Healthcare Associates, the biggest women's healthcare provider in the Portland area. It's one of a small but growing number of birth centers operated by physician/midwife groups. The Portland group already had agreements with most insurers in the area—and with the state Medicaid program—which made it easy for them to get on the list of "preferred" birth centers. Another economic advantage over traditional birth centers is that all patient care can be kept under the group umbrella: when women have to be transferred to a physician's care, the midwives are backed up by doctors from the same practice.

It's also good for the patients, says Nora Tallman, one of the six certified nurse-midwives who staff the birth center. "I trust the doctors I consult with and refer to because I know they are on our side," she says.

Midwifery Birth Center is a low-slung building on the edge of a suburban strip mall. The lobby is shared with a busy women's clinic. But beyond the doors that separate birth center and clinic, a peaceful feeling prevails. The furnishings are mostly modern, with the obligatory kitchen and family room and a series of suites. Each is spacious, with big tubs for laboring—but not for birth, under the facility's rules.

Tallman has worked as a home birth midwife and in

a hospital, and she prefers the birth center. "It is really a lovely merging of the worlds," she says. "I would love to see this model as the future of birth centers." If a woman Tallman transfers to a nearby hospital simply needs drugs to kick-start labor, the same team of midwives can administer them and retain control through the entire birth. If the woman needs more, like a vacuum-assisted delivery or a D&C to stop bleeding, Tallman reaches out to whichever of her physician colleagues is on call.

Women get their prenatal exams in the birthing suites, so they will be familiar with the different spaces and can pick the one they like best. The nurses who take their blood pressure and draw blood are the same nurses who will help with their births. "In most hospital practices women come into a room they've never been in before, and they're taken care of by nurses they've never met before," Tallman says.

Tucked in the corner of one suite is a portable wooden birthing stool that Tallman lugged all over the state when she was attending home births and putting a thousand miles a month on her car. It's got a padded seat and folds up for easy carrying. Some women like to use it during the pushing stage, because it supports them as they squat. The center has a full array of other birthing aids, from big balls to peanut-shaped pillows that help support women laboring on their sides. Hooks on the ceilings accommodate yoga slings.

Midwifery Birth Center is unusual in offering its own childbirth classes, but education is a passion for Tallman. She wrote a book called *The Inner Work of Birth* to help women prepare for the transition to motherhood and learn to overcome their fears. "We talk about what I call the 'impossible point' in labor, when people think, 'I can't do it anymore. I've reached my limit.'" Tallman encourages women to let go of the belief that they can only endure so much. "I'll say, 'Go into a place where you are extraordinary, where you can do anything,'" she says. "It's not that you make the pain hurt less, it's that you've reached a new level of coping ability within yourself."

Another class focuses on what happens when a couple doesn't get the birth they want. Participants meet one of the group's obstetricians and discuss how to adapt if circumstances derail their dreams of a physiologic birth.

Working in a birth center has been a rejuvenating experience for Tallman, who's been catching babies for forty-one years. She hasn't lost her enthusiasm for birth—or for midwifery, which she's convinced can change the world, one mother and baby at a time.

"When a mother sees her birth as an empowering experience or an experience that intensified her bond with her partner or her sense of maturation as a woman," she says, "it makes her into a better mother for that baby, and I think that very strongly affects how that child is raised."

10

"Do you want to discuss the birth?" Kopas asks. "Close the door."

She's huddled in the tiny midwives' room at the hospital with Andrea Humphrey, a midwifery student at the University of Washington. They've just helped a woman named Layla deliver her first child after nearly two days of labor, culminating in a four-and-a-half-hour marathon of pushing. The exhausted mother and baby are resting. The midwives are catching their breaths before moving on to the next patient.

"How do you feel about it?" Kopas asks the student.

"I felt it went pretty well," Humphrey says. "The actual birth was really fast, the baby cried right away, there was a little bleeding, but not much."

"What would you have done differently?" Kopas asks.

Humphrey is in her third year, just months from graduation. She's wrapping up the clinical part of her education, the part where students work side by side with veteran mid-wives. The amount of hands-on opportunity students get depends on the individual preceptors. Kopas guides students when they seem uncertain but lets them take the lead when she thinks they're ready. After deliveries, she debriefs with observations and advice—never criticism.

"Mary Lou is a powerhouse," says Katherine Teela Zeichner, one of many younger midwives in Washington who draw on lessons learned from Kopas. "I feel lucky to have been her student."

Kopas let Zeichner spend time alone with clients at the start of their clinic visits to get acquainted with them and learn how to chart. She gave Zeichner the freedom to sit with women during labor on her own. "It gave me a lot of confidence to be able to work with patients one-on-one," says Zeichner, now a midwife at Kaiser Permanente. When she badly misjudged one patient's cervical dilation—that tricky estimate made by bridging the opening with two fingers—Kopas didn't make her feel worse than she already did. "It was a very rookie mess-up, and I was really appreciative that Mary Lou didn't make it seem like I had made a huge mistake."

During emergencies, Kopas took charge—but also taught

by example how to stay cool in a crisis. Zeichner stood in a corner and watched one nasty postpartum hemorrhage unfold. "There was so much blood," she says. "I remember Mary Lou putting her entire arm in the woman's vagina and compressing down on her abdomen with her other hand. I'm sure she was scared, but she seemed calm and did everything she should have."

Being able to think clearly in critical situations is a skill every midwife must possess, and it is something preceptors look for as they gauge each student's suitability for the job. Ann Olsen, the home birth midwife, had a student who passed out when a woman started to bleed heavily. Nora Tallman, the birth center midwife, has seen students freeze up. "You have to have the ability to lead, to be the rock of Gibraltar when the shit hits the fan," she says. Zeichner credits Kopas for helping her develop that ability. "I do feel like I'm pretty calm during emergencies, and a lot of that stems back to Mary Lou and seeing how she handled those situations."

When Zeichner and Kopas worked call shifts together, they both slept in the midwives' room—Kopas in the bed, the student two feet away on a recliner that folds flat. Previous students had tried to make the hard vinyl more comfortable with a foam mattress topper cut to fit. It wasn't great, but it wasn't the worst sleeping situation Zeichner encountered during her clinical rotations. As the person with the least standing, she often had no place to lie down when the bunkroom at another hospital was full.

Humphrey also shares the tiny quarters at UW Medical Center–Northwest with the on-call midwife. Like most midwifery students at the UW, she was already a registered nurse when she started the program. Some schools offer an accelerated nursing education for people who already have a degree in another field. The midwifery graduate program itself is usually a two-year master's degree. But several schools, including the UW, have shifted to a three-year doctoral program—over the objections of the American College of Nurse-Midwives. The organization argues that the higher degree is more costly as well as unnecessary for people who just want to practice midwifery. But Humphrey appreciates the extra emphasis on policy and research.

As a labor and delivery nurse, she has been present for hundreds of births, but never as the person in charge. One of the new skills she's learning is how to stitch up torn perineal tissue. She started with yarn and foam, then graduated to rubbery, fake vaginas. She and her fellow students even practice on chicken legs. Partly because she pushed for so long, Layla, the woman who just gave birth, experienced a third-degree tear—a serious injury where the rip extends into the muscles that surround the anus. It's rare, and hospital protocol calls for a surgeon to get involved.

In Layla's case, the obstetrician stitched the anal muscles, then handed responsibility back to the midwives. Kopas has fond memories of a preceptor who allowed her to repair a tear on her own, even though as a student she was slow and clumsy at first. Kopas gave Humphrey the same chance, letting her stitch up the wound. Since Layla had an epidural, pain wasn't an issue.

Now Kopas reviews the distinction between second- and third-degree tears, to be sure Humphrey can recognize the difference. She also offers tips on how to hold the needle for a cleaner stitch. But, she adds, it's even better to prevent tears in the first place, which means helping guide the baby's head out slowly.

By keeping your hands on the perineum and feeling the bulge, it's possible to anticipate the head's emergence, Kopas explains. "I definitely think if you can avoid that pop of the head, you don't get as much tearing. When you feel the head coming you can tell the woman to slow down, not push."

Kopas praises the way Humphrey connected with Layla, who was initially wary of having a student at her birth. "You came in really friendly and confident," Kopas says. "I think that's how you carry yourself, and it's genuine. It's not put on, and people can sense that."

After filling out charts and eating their sack lunches, Kopas and Humphrey return to Layla's room to check on her and her husband and do the newborn exam on their daughter. It's been a few hours, and families are always eager to talk about the momentous experience they just went through, Kopas explains. It's particularly valuable for women who had difficult labors or interventions they didn't plan, and she likes to initiate a free-ranging conversation to help them process everything that's happened and how they feel about it.

She and Humphrey sit and chat with Layla and her husband like old friends. They talk about how the couple met. How long it took them to decide to have a baby. In a way, the four really are friends, at least in the moment—bonded by an intense, life-changing event.

"Was it what you expected?" Humphrey asks.

Layla and her husband look at each other and laugh. She

says she had no idea what to expect. He says he didn't think it would take so long.

"You were on the longer end," Humphrey confirms. "Four and a half hours—with success!"

For much of that time, the baby was faceup instead of the normal, facedown presentation. Kopas tried to turn the baby with her hands, but it kept flipping back. Later, with Layla on her hands and knees, the baby turned on its own. At one point, Humphrey gave the discouraged woman a mirror so she could see that the baby's head actually was beginning to emerge.

"I remember you saying, 'Women's bodies! So amazing!'" Humphrey recalls, nodding in concurrence with the sense of wonder.

The baby is nursing, and a feeling of drowsy contentment pervades the room.

"This should pretty much be it for the next few days," Kopas says, gesturing to encompass the scene of mother and baby in bed, with dad close at hand. "The baby is going to want to nurse and sleep. When she sleeps, you sleep.

"Do you have any other questions?"

Layla shakes her head no. "Thank you, guys. You were the dream team."

It's the kind of conclusion midwives strive for—a healthy mom, a healthy baby, and a birth experience the family feels good about.

But not all pregnancies are trouble-free. Not all birth stories have a happy ending.

K opas and Humphrey are together again, this time in the clinic for a day of patient visits.

If catching babies is the icing on the cake for midwives, building relationships with women and their families is the bread and butter. For many, it's the heart of the job.

"We're all birth addicts," says midwife Cindy Rogers, one of Kopas's partners at UW. "There's this huge wave of energy that comes out at you when a baby is born. . . . But for me the essence of midwifery is that intimacy with people, providing emotional support and seeing people grow over time and being with them."

Humphrey, thirty-three, has a lot of experience connecting with women in her job as a nurse, but those are fleeting relationships. Now in her clinical rotations she's getting the chance to meet women and learn about their lives and concerns long before their due dates. The UW group is especially nice, because the midwives are able to spend more time with their clients than midwives at some of the other sites where she has also trained, Humphrey says.

"This is the kind of place I would like to deliver my own baby someday."

Midway through the morning, Humphrey and Kopas meet with a young couple named Gina and Dominic. It's their first pregnancy and their first visit to the midwives' clinic. Initial appointments last at least an hour, so everyone can get acquainted. The midwife takes a detailed medical history, and the woman and her family have a chance to explain their hopes and concerns. Prospective parents can also experience that first ultrasound—the magical moment when they see their baby-to-be and leave with snapshots in hand.

Gina estimates she's about nine to ten weeks along. "I'm a normal level of anxious," she tells the midwives when they ask about her state of mind. She's got a range of health problems, including migraines. But she's buzzing with excitement about being pregnant. She and Dominic have been watching episodes of *Call the Midwife* every night.

Gina's most pressing concern at the moment is nausea.

"I feel queasy all the time. Food doesn't sound good," she says.

Humphrey suggests the old standbys, crackers and carbonated beverages, but says she can also prescribe medications if Gina needs them. Kopas suggests magnesium supplements as a migraine preventative. They discuss genetic screening for birth defects, which the couple is keen on. They don't want to know the baby's sex in advance.

"I feel like it's the last surprise I will ever have in my entire life," Gina says, laughing and serious at the same time.

The visit is nearing its end when Kopas asks if they want the ultrasound exam.

"Oh, yes!" Dominic says, emphatically. "We're having the ultrasound."

Humphrey starts with the handheld Doppler, to see if it can pick up the heartbeat. "It can be tricky to find this early," she says, as the instrument remains silent. "The baby is very small. I'm not concerned."

Kopas switches on the clinic's more powerful ultrasound machine. Scans at such an early stage require expertise on the part of the operator, which Kopas gained through special training. She presses the wand to Gina's lower abdomen. A blurry image about the size and shape of a bean swims into focus. "This is the baby," Kopas says. It's about an inch long, right on track for its gestational age. But she can't locate the tiny, pulsating blip of a heart either. "So far it looks fine," she says, cautiously. "I just can't see it very well." Kopas suggests a transvaginal ultrasound, which can produce a sharper image from a probe inserted into the vagina. Gina slips off her bottoms while Kopas prepares the machine, lubricating the probe with clear, bluish gel.

The image pops into focus on the screen, clear and distinct. Kopas points out the tadpole-like fetus and its attached yolk sac, floating in an amniotic bubble. "It definitely looks like a nine-week fetus to me," she says. But no beating heart is visible. She moves the wand to capture images from every possible angle, then tries again. Still nothing. Kopas withdraws the probe.

"Are heartbeats normally easy to see at this stage?" Gina asks, sitting up. She doesn't sound worried yet. Just curious.

Kopas chooses her words carefully. She's had to break this news before, and it never gets easier.

"Ordinarily it's really easy to see," she says. "So, it's worrisome to me that we're not seeing it."

She pauses.

"Clearly, that's a baby. I don't know if it's still growing."

Kopas never says the fetus is dead. She would need more confirmatory tests to be certain. But the midwife knows this baby will never be born. She repeats herself to be sure the couple understand: if there was a heartbeat, the ultrasound would see it. She offers to schedule a radiology consultation for a definitive answer.

The room is silent as the couple absorb the message.

Gina draws in a shaky breath. Her shoulders heave with a single, strangled sob. Then she composes herself and straightens her back. She works in a women's clinic and knows what comes next.

"I get it," she says. "D&C?"

Kopas hugs her. "I'm so sorry. We don't have a good answer for why this happens. You didn't do anything wrong. But that doesn't make it easier."

Gina's gaze drifts across the room to the image of the fetus, still frozen on the ultrasound screen.

"Can I have the picture?" she asks.

MIDWIVES CALL IT A nonviability, or early pregnancy loss. It happens in about 10 percent of pregnancies, mostly in the first trimester. Helping women cope with miscarriage and its emotional toll is part of every midwife's job.

Much rarer are the cases where a baby dies shortly before

or after birth. Genetic abnormalities are often to blame, but sometimes there's no explanation—which can be even more distressing. As a nurse, Kopas helped women deliver fetuses born so early they never drew breath, as well as babies with such severe abnormalities that death was inevitable. The clinical term is "incompatible with life." Perhaps the most devastating situations midwives and their patients encounter are termed "demises"—full-term babies that die in the womb.

A woman whose fetus was fine the week before comes in for one of her final checkups and there's no heartbeat. "I remember the first time it happened," Kopas says. She searched and searched and was stunned to find no sign of life. "I was upset, with tears in my eyes. And the woman is crying and saying, 'Why is this happening?' The only answer I had was 'I don't know.'"

After the shock of discovering her baby has died, the woman then faces the almost unimaginable ordeal of delivering the dead infant. The midwife's duty is to be with her throughout the process.

"It's always terrible to have to say, 'Your baby has died,'" says Rogers, who has more experience of these cases than Kopas or any of their other partners. "That's one of the crappiest parts of this job. But midwifery is saying, 'I'm going to walk through this darkness with you. I'm here, and I care about you.'"

Women often want to hold their baby and have pictures taken. Sometimes, after the body has been moved to the hospital morgue, a woman asks to see it again. "If that's what she wants, you go get it," Kopas says. "There's nothing we can do to change the situation, but we bend over backwards to do whatever she needs."

Most of all, Kopas has found, a woman facing the worst heartbreak of her life needs a steady, reassuring presence by her side. "You want to be sensitive, but you can't be falling apart. That's not what she needs. She needs somebody strong and comforting." That's especially true during and after the delivery. "People are so scared of seeing their baby. The most terrifying thing to them is that they don't know what it's going to look like. Just being the person there who is matter-of-fact about it, who's comfortable with it—that's what they need."

The parents aren't the only ones who carry the scars from those tragedies. Empathy is essential to being a midwife. But it also opens the heart and mind to pain. One analysis estimates hospital midwives encounter at least a dozen traumatic situations every year. Another study ranks the level of burnout among midwives second only to that of prison officials. Sometimes a single bad experience is enough to scare people away from the profession.

Early in her first midwifery job, one of Kopas's partners at UW was confronted with a full-term stillbirth and two massive postpartum hemorrhages in quick succession. In one case, the woman started bleeding profusely as she was pushing the baby out. An obstetrician took control, but the woman nearly died in the operating room. The young midwife felt helpless.

"The worst part of it for me was that I felt like there was nothing I could do," she recalls. For a long time afterward, she felt a sense of dread every time she delivered a placenta. Would this woman also start bleeding uncontrollably? She began having heart palpitations. It was a psychiatric nurse-practitioner who helped her cope and recognize that what she was experiencing was the physical manifestations of stress.

FEW MIDWIVES IN THE United States will ever see a woman die in childbirth. But Humphrey plans to put her degree to work in the developing world, where pregnancy can be far more perilous. A few weeks before starting her clinical rotation with Kopas, she spent a weekend at a workshop run by PRONTO International, a nonprofit that stages realistic simulations of obstetrical and neonatal emergencies to train medical workers in places like Kenya, Uganda, and India. Volunteers wearing pants with built-in vaginas, rectums, and bags filled with fake blood, act out a range of crises, from hemorrhage to babies that aren't breathing. One of the simulations Humphrey participated in involved a woman in labor whose blood pressure was spiking while her worried mother loudly demanded to know what was going on.

International midwifery is a growing field. Midwives from the United States find jobs or volunteer with international aid organizations, disaster relief programs, and missionary groups. Humphrey did a stint as a nurse in a massive refugee camp in South Sudan, working for Doctors Without Borders. During the days, she helped at health clinics. In the evenings, she hung out in a maternity tent where midwives from Kenya, Holland, and Ethiopia delivered as many as three hundred babies a month.

"It was this powerful environment, all women," Humphrey says. Women shed their headscarves and inhibitions and helped each other through labor. A Dutch midwife shared information about birth control, biology, and women's empowerment with the refugee women who visited the maternity tent. With no real operating room, C-sections were extreme emergencies, performed only to save the mother—not the baby.

Every midwife has to deal with unpredictable situations, but working in a low-income country requires another level of flexibility and problem-solving. "You have to be comfortable being uncomfortable," says Diana Garde, a CNM working in Bangladesh at the world's largest refugee camp. "You have to be OK with being hot and dehydrated and not having flush toilets or toilet paper or familiar foods."

Garde's first international experience was in the midst of an Ebola epidemic in Sierra Leone. She was hired by the global health organization Partners in Health to help run an isolation center for pregnant women suspected of having the virus. They couldn't be admitted to the regular maternity ward until tests came back negative. Women who tested positive were supposed to be transferred to an Ebola treatment unit. One pregnant woman with Ebola was bleeding so heavily, the staff knew she wouldn't survive the trip, so they kept her in the unit and provided supportive care until she died. Another woman delivered her baby, then bled out through her IV. Few babies born to infected mothers survived.

"I've seen more maternal deaths and stillbirths than I'd ever care to see in a lifetime," Garde says.

But she and her colleagues were able to train local nurses to handle a wider range of obstetrical emergencies for women who weren't infected—things like obstructed labor or the seizures caused by high blood pressure called eclampsia. She also spent a year in Uganda, teaching at the country's first bachelor-level midwifery program. The students fanned out to rural health posts for their clinical experience, and she monitored their deliveries and follow-up care. At one clinic, Garde and the students were sitting on the lawn watching a video about breech presentation when they heard "a kerfuffle, like a bunch of hens in a yard," she recalls. A woman had gone into labor on the grass, and other women had formed a circle, shielding her from view with their wraps. The students rushed over and helped deliver the baby. "It was a beautiful moment. A beautiful little girl."

In Bangladesh, Garde works for the World Health Organization to improve care for displaced women and girls and advocate for reproductive health rights. Nearly one million

Rohingya refugees have been living in the sprawling complex since the government of Myanmar attacked the country's Muslim minority communities. "I think maybe I've found the perfect job for myself," Garde says. "Problem-solving and being able to look at the big picture is really stimulating."

She lives in a hotel and works in an office in the same building. It's a contract-to-contract existence. Garde doesn't know how long her job will last, so she's already casting around for other options. "At some point in my life, I would like to have a kitchen and yard again," she says. "But it's a little hard for me to think about finding a job at home that fills me the way that this does."

Humphrey feels the same.

"My big drive in being a midwife is to reduce maternal mortality, to have women be more aware of their bodies and have access to contraceptives," she says. "I would like to begin with the women who have the least rights, and those are refugee women. This feels like the place where I can have the most worthwhile contribution."

Other members of midwifery's next generation are focusing their energy closer to home—on the racial and health inequities that persist in the United States.

Marilyn Acquah is a labor and delivery nurse who has worked in hospitals for years. She knows her way around the medical system. But she's not at all confident about her own prospects for a safe, uncomplicated pregnancy within that system.

Though she's not currently pregnant, it's a subject she and her other black friends discuss a lot, in light of statistics that show they're much more likely than white women to experience problems—or even die—during childbirth. "There's this trepidation about what kind of care they're going to get, where they should have their babies, whether they're going to encounter conflicts with doctors," says Acquah, who's also a first-year midwifery student at the University of Washington. "Just because I'm a medical professional, there's no reason to expect I would be an exception. If you look at the data, it cuts across socioeconomic levels. It doesn't matter your education."

Even superstars aren't immune. Beyoncé suffered

preeclampsia, a combination of high blood pressure and toxic levels of protein in the blood that led to an emergency C-section when her twins were born in 2017. Tennis champion Serena Williams developed blood clots in her lungs after her daughter's birth. When she complained of shortness of breath and asked to be checked, hospital staff initially brushed her off.

"If women like that cannot be heard and listened to, who am I?" Acquah asks.

As study after study has shown, midwifery care offers at least a partial solution to the disparities in outcomes in the United States. That's why, at the age of thirty-five, Acquah is devoting three years and more than eighty thousand dollars in tuition to earning a doctorate in the field.

"It's a passion for me to do more to address that maternal mortality rate. It's an area where I feel like I can make a difference," she says, in a Seattle coffee shop on one of the rare days when she isn't in class or working a twelve-hour nursing shift. Balancing the heavy workload of a doctoral program with the typical grind of long nursing shifts has been a challenge. "It's an expensive leap of faith. When I got in, I was so happy, but I've also never cried so much in my life because of this huge decision."

Part of Acquah's apprehension is about joining a profession hampered by its own homogeneity. In a country where nearly half of babies are born to women of color, more than 90 percent of nurse-midwives are white. Fewer than 2 percent are men, and only a handful identify as transgender.

One of Acquah's friends abandoned a career in midwifery because she felt she was likely to be judged more harshly and receive less support from colleagues and bosses. Acquah knows what it's like to be one of the few. At the hospital where she works, only about 1 percent of labor and delivery nurses are black.

"It's hard to be in all-white spaces," she says. "I feel like there's a burden to be the best, and there's also not a lot of leeway to make mistakes without that reflecting on you and the other black people there."

Racism was an undercurrent at nurse-midwifery's beginnings, when Mary Breckinridge portrayed the whites of Appalachia as true Americans more deserving of care than immigrants or African Americans. Racism was also inherent in the campaign to eradicate granny and immigrant midwives.

Breckinridge came from a Confederate family and "spoke with kindness about the freed slaves with whom she was raised," writes historian Laura Ettinger. But she wouldn't dine with African Americans. As late as the 1960s, her Frontier Nursing Service refused to hire black nurses. When Breckinridge organized the first professional association for nurse-midwives, minority women were not welcome.

The American College of Nurse-Midwives was founded in 1955 partly to shake off those racist roots, and the organization's leadership has made diversity a top priority in recent years. Sessions on racism and health disparities are featured at every midwifery conference, and the group is working to eliminate bias in education. A diversity and inclusion task force that surveyed members revealed the way midwives of color often feel marginalized at the same time that they are expected to educate their white colleagues and lead efforts to increase diversity. ACNM offers scholarships and mentoring programs for students of color, says Felina Ortiz, who chairs the organization's Midwives of Color Committee. An assistant professor at the University of New Mexico's College of Nursing, Ortiz is a first-generation college graduate whose ancestors include a traditional *partera*, or midwife. She's working to make the midwifery curriculum more inclusive and accepting of cultural differences—while still maintaining its scientific rigor. Some Native American and Hispanic students, for example, are reluctant to discuss cancer risk, because many of their patients share a common belief that talking about bad things can make them happen. So Ortiz coaches students to broach the subject in terms of a third person.

Many midwifery schools have policies to encourage people of color to apply, and to support them. A quarter of new midwifery students nationwide are people of color, and attrition rates are dropping. About 15 percent of newly minted nurse-midwives are people of color.

Increasing diversity among midwives is a matter of survival for the profession—and the best way to improve the health of women and babies of all races and cultures. The one-on-one care midwives provide is most effective when caregiver and patient share a common background. Outcomes are generally better, because communication and trust are easier to establish.

"I know what I feel like when I have a provider who looks like me," Acquah says. "It makes a big difference."

SOME MIDWIVES ARE PIONEERING care tailored for, and provided by, people of color. Tara Lawal, who has a master's degree in midwifery and is working on a doctorate in nursing practice, founded and serves as executive director of Rainier Valley Midwives in Seattle. The group serves women of all backgrounds, including large numbers of immigrants. Their small clinic feels more like a high-end spa than a medical office, with couches, brightly colored tapestries draped from the ceiling, and screened-off nooks for exams. It's a welcoming environment where women feel comfortable—which also means they are more likely to open up and less likely to skip appointments.

Lawal, who spends much of her time applying for grants, has won funding to build a birth center and offer group prenatal care and pregnancy classes modeled after a March of Dimes program in Memphis that virtually eliminated C-sections among the mainly low-income black women who participated. "We choose midwives from within the communities we serve, in order to give women culturally appropriate care that matches who they are, where they come from, and what happens to them into parenthood," says Lawal, who has cultural roots in Hawaii and India.

The Rainier Valley Midwives are a mix of CNMs and CPMs. One of them is Faisa Farole, who emigrated with her family from Somalia when she was nine.

Before she became a midwife, Farole worked as a medical

interpreter and doula for Somali families and saw how often miscommunication and cultural insensitivity led to unwanted inductions or C-sections. She decided to become a certified professional midwife so she could help women give birth at home free from pressure and technological interventions. But most of her Somali clients view home birth as old-fashioned. They want their babies to be born in hospitals, with doctors and all the assurances Western medicine can offer.

So Lawal and Farole are pioneering an innovative approach they call the "birth bundle," which marries community midwifery with hospital delivery. Women receive intensive prenatal care from midwives of color, then give birth in the hospital under the care of physicians who have also spent time at the midwives' clinic. Farole and other midwives stay with their clients in the hospital, acting as advisers and advocates. It's impossible to overestimate the value of having a caregiver from the same culture, especially during an event as intimate as birth, she says. "It just melts the suspicion. There is so much trust that happens. The mom knows that I am looking out for her own good. That I am on her side."

Sometimes Farole helps women avoid unnecessary interventions. Sometimes she explains to them why their safest option is surgical delivery. "The mother might be refusing to have a C-section because when she's back home, she has nobody to look after her and the other kids," Farole says. "I know what she's worried about and where her mind is, but I also know that the baby's heart rate is going down and what the doctors are saying is valid."

Farole also has a thriving home birth practice. Many of her clients are black or Latina women leery of the medical establishment and willing to drive two hours or more from surrounding communities to be cared for by a midwife of color.

The ranks of CPMs are slightly more diverse than those of certified nurse-midwives, but more than 80 percent are white women. Men remain the rarest minority in both branches of the profession. Ira Kantrowitz-Gordon, who directs the University of Washington's midwifery education program, was the only man in his class when he graduated in 1998—and no others have yet followed in his footsteps.

Finding a practice willing to hire him took a long time, and some of his female colleagues were not thrilled. "I just set out to prove I could be a sensitive, caring practitioner," he says. "That's what most people want—not necessarily a woman." He occasionally encounters a patient who doesn't want to be cared for by a man, but it's rare.

Simon Adriane Ellis got his first taste of birth when his best friend delivered before she could make it to the hospital. Ellis was by her side. "It was the most beautiful human experience I ever witnessed in my life," he recalls. Ellis chose midwifery as a career soon after transitioning from female to male. Administrators at the first school he applied to were baffled and told him they weren't sure they could find any preceptors willing to train him. "The easiest part was working with the patients," he says. "The hardest part was everybody else's idea that patients wouldn't want to work with a man."

Ellis is now a CNM at Kaiser Permanente. As one of the country's few transgender midwives, he particularly enjoys helping trans and nonbinary people work through fertility treatment, conception, and birth.

"They feel more comfortable with me, so they're more likely to open up."

The first time she gave birth, Jessica Jones did it with very little technology: minimal medical interventions, no pain meds, except a few puffs of nitrous oxide that didn't do anything. Just her own body, intense determination, and the support of her husband, doula, and midwife.

This time around, she's getting the works.

Jones didn't plan it that way, but as Kopas always warns her clients, "You never know what kind of labor the universe is going to give you."

Jones's first son arrived on his due date. Son number two is taking his time—so much so that she and her husband, Tim, reluctantly decide to induce labor. Nearly a quarter of women in the United States make the same choice. Some do it as a matter of convenience. Midwives recommend induction only for the safety of mother or child—though making the call isn't always clear-cut. Jones and Kopas discuss the trade-offs several times. They keep coming back to the

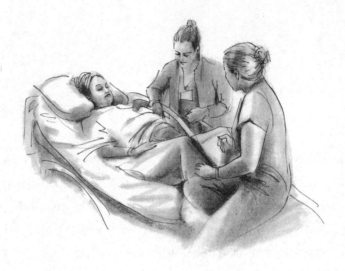

epidemiological data showing pregnancies that drag on too long can be dangerous for the fetus.

At full term, or thirty-nine weeks of gestation, babies are ready to live outside the womb. The longer they stay in the mother's body, the higher the chance of problems as the placenta begins to deteriorate. Particularly for women over the age of thirty-five, incidence of stillbirths rises sharply past the fortieth week. Though the risks are still small, the correlation is so strong that some obstetricians advocate inducing every woman at thirty-nine weeks. Under the protocol Kopas and her group agreed on at their recent team meeting, they offer induction at forty weeks for older mothers and recommend it at forty-one weeks.

Most women who go past their due dates are so sick of being pregnant they'll try almost anything to get the ball rolling. Short of induction, there's no surefire method to bring on labor, but midwives offer a small repertoire of tips. Having sex is a time-honored technique with no downside, but there's also no evidence it works. Kopas doesn't recommend castor oil, but some midwives swear by it. Nipple stimulation releases the contraction-triggering hormone oxytocin and has been shown to have a slight effect. In the final weeks of her pregnancy, Jones underwent two membrane sweeps, a procedure where the midwife inserts a finger into the cervix to separate the bag that holds the baby from the uterine wall. The process stimulates secretion of prostaglandins, chemicals that cause the cervix to soften and thin and can promote contractions. For Jones, it was uncomfortable and didn't seem to make much of a difference.

An archivist who loves research, history, and storytelling, Jones is also a believer in evidence-based medicine. Just months away from her fortieth birthday, she's well within the "older moms" category. One of her friends lost a baby at full term due to preeclampsia, so she knows terrible things really can happen. Forty-one weeks and three days into her pregnancy, Jones and her husband check into the hospital at 8 a.m. Before the day is through, she will experience many of the interventions midwives and their clients usually try to avoid: being hooked to an IV; epidural pain relief; having her water broken manually; and continuous fetal monitoring. She'll also suffer a frightening complication. It won't be the kind of birth most people associate with midwifery, but it will exemplify the midwifery model of care. At every step, Jones and her husband will get to make the choices, with Kopas to guide and support them. "Despite the complication and everything else, it was a good experience," Jones said several weeks later. "It was never just about the mechanics of what was going to happen. It was also about how we were feeling and what our mental state was."

The day begins with the question of how best to nudge Jones's body into labor. Kopas runs through options, starting with the most conservative: inserting a bulb into the cervical opening to promote dilation. "It's like a water balloon sitting inside your cervix, and it just exerts a little pressure," Kopas explains. "It inflates to about the size of an egg."

Jones agrees to give it a try.

The procedure doesn't go well. It's painful and Kopas

can't get the device firmly lodged. Jones's cervix is so soft—or "ripe"—that the bulb keeps falling out.

That's a promising sign her body is progressing toward labor. Kopas says it's probably time for intravenous Pitocin, the synthetic form of oxytocin commonly used to induce labor. New evidence shows induction doesn't normally raise the risk of C-sections for healthy women with low-risk pregnancies. But the drug can trigger such frequent contractions that the baby becomes stressed, Kopas explains. Because of that, Jones will have to stay tethered to a fetal heart monitor. An IV makes it easy to adjust the dose, starting low and ratcheting up if necessary.

"There's nothing that's perfect," Kopas cautions. "It's not a predictable business. We'll just see how your body does." Every baby's birth is different, she adds. This one clearly isn't going to be like his brother's; it's going to be all his own.

A couple of hours later, Jones is sitting on a blue birthing ball, riding out sporadic contractions. She's wearing a hospital gown, and her short brown hair is tucked behind her ears. Her spasms still aren't regular. The next step is manually breaking her bag of water, which often speeds things up, Kopas explains. Jones is ready. She's also getting worried about pain.

It's been several weeks since Jones got any decent sleep. She's been bedeviled by insomnia, migraine headaches, random contractions, and the general misery of feeling like a bloated cow. Her first labor dragged on more than nineteen hours. The prospect of going through that again without drugs is losing its appeal.

She and Kopas discuss the pros and cons of an epidural.

Jones can have the procedure at any point in the process, Kopas says. Once the anesthesiologist inserts the catheter in her back, she won't be able to get out of bed. She can't eat anything, either—though she's not exactly in a snacking mood. It's really just a question of what she wants. "Labor is an altered mental state," Kopas says, perched on a stool at the foot of Jones's bed. "There's going to be some intensity to go through before you have this baby, there's no getting around it. You did it unmedicated the last time, and it was a great experience, so you know what that's like. If you want to try it again, I'll be here helping you through it. If you want a different experience, where you're not in as much pain, go for the epidural.

"But don't do it for anyone but yourself, because it's your choice."

That's all Jones needs to hear. Tension drains from her body as she relaxes into the decision she was already leaning toward. "I'm OK with saying, 'Thanks for modern medicine,'" she says. "I don't have anything to prove."

The anesthesiologist is summoned.

Tall and friendly, he runs through the procedure and tells Jones what to expect. At his direction, she sits on the edge of the bed, leans forward, and hunches her back, while Tim kneels at her feet and holds her hands. A needle is slipped between vertebra. A catheter no bigger than a fishing line is inserted and connected to the IV pump. The first dose flows at the push of a button. Jones closes her eyes and sighs.

When the drug takes hold, Kopas breaks Jones's water with an instrument that looks like a crochet hook. She checks the cervix: five centimeters and 80 percent effaced. The baby's heart rate is strong.

The bustle in the room dies down. Kopas leaves to tend to her record keeping. She hopes Jones will be able to sleep for a while. But an hour later, the baby's heart rate takes a nosedive. Kopas hurries back to the room. The tracing recovers and stays in the normal range. Jones is at seven centimeters, 90 percent effaced.

At 8:30 p.m., there's a rush of bloody show—a thick vaginal discharge of blood and mucus that can presage labor. Jones is a sliver short of full dilation. She tries pushing, but the baby doesn't budge. Despite the epidural, Jones is also feeling the pain of contractions, so the anesthesiologist returns to bump up the dosage. Kopas retreats again and waits—something midwives are very good at.

More than fourteen hours after Jones and her husband arrived at the hospital, her biological cylinders start to click. Contractions are strong and steady. The pain still isn't completely vanquished, though. Lying on her side with pillows under her head and shoulders, Jones breathes heavily, her belly rising and falling.

An epidural can make labor less excruciating, but it doesn't allow women to relax and wait for the baby to appear. Barring a C-section, every woman has to push her baby out, and it's rarely easy. For women with an epidural, Kopas takes a more active, coaching role because the anesthetic can blunt the overwhelming urge to push and the sensation of forcing the baby down. She will even insert her fingers to gauge progress—something she never does during a physiologic birth.

"Take a deep breath," she urges Jones. "Hold it and push—right down into your bottom." Jones grabs her knees and pulls back, leveraging herself and opening her pelvis. "That's good," Kopas says. "That's it. You're doing it."

Between pushes, Tim serves his wife sips of water through a straw and kisses the top of her head.

As the pace picks up, Kopas and Jones hit a stride. The epidural finally begins to numb her lower half, so Jones feels the pressure, but not the intense pain, of the contractions. Kopas helps Jones connect with the rhythm. "More pressure. More pressure," the midwife chants. She checks the baby's motion. "Do that again. Yes! Really hard!"

Jones is puffing and groaning. Kopas grabs her hand and Jones pulls back against the midwife's weight. "That's good! That's good!" Kopas says, almost growling. "Keep it coming."

The bassinet is ready, with the warming lights on and flannel blankets neatly stacked.

Ten more pushes and the baby is crowning.

"Great job," Kopas says. Her voice drops. "Little pushes now, little, little, little."

Then he's out—a long, lean boy named Samuel.

He's pink and breathing flawlessly but barely cries. Deposited on his mother's chest, he regards her solemnly. All action in the room is briefly suspended as everyone takes in the tableau of mother and child. Then the bustle resumes. Tim wraps his wife and son in his arms and snaps pictures. Samuel squirms and mews, as if trying to converse. Kopas helps Jones deliver the placenta then quickly stitches up a second-degree laceration. Samuel noses his way to a nipple and latches on. Everything seems fine by the time the midwife quietly exits.

Kopas is nearly done with her charting when the nurse sounds the alarm. Jones is bleeding heavily.

Postpartum hemorrhage strikes about 3 percent of women in the United States and is the leading cause of maternal mortality. Though deaths are rare in the developed world, hemorrhage rates have been increasing for reasons that aren't clear.

Jones is dizzy, nauseated, and pale. Blood soaks the pads beneath her. The lights are up and the peaceful mood shattered as Kopas and the nurse launch into action like the well-practiced team they are. They check Jones's blood pressure, hook up another IV, and switch her epidural back on. What comes next is going to hurt. Jones also gets a dose of fentanyl, a powerful, fast-acting narcotic.

One of the most common causes of hemorrhage is what midwives call a boggy uterus—one that fails to constrict after expelling the placenta. But when Kopas presses on Jones's abdomen, it feels firm. Another possibility is a knot of coagulated blood lodged inside the neck of the organ, preventing it from closing. Kopas reaches in almost to her elbow. She doesn't feel any retained placenta but pulls out a handful of reddish-black clots.

There's an arsenal of drugs to make the uterus contract and promote coagulation. Over the next hour, Jones gets most of them: Pitocin, Methergine, misoprostol, Hemabate, tranexamic acid. It's an urgent situation, but Kopas takes the time to explain each medication and how it works. Soon the medical bombardment seems to take effect. The bleeding slows, then stops.

Less than an hour later, blood starts gushing again.

Kopas extracts another fistful of clots and orders a second round of medication. She calls the on-duty obstetrician. The doctor attempts to insert a device called a uterine balloon—which is exactly what it sounds like. Placed inside the uterus, then inflated with water, the balloon presses against the organ walls and cuts off bleeding. But the device won't stay in place. At that point, even without the balloon, the bleeding diminishes to a trickle, then stops.

Jones has lost nearly two and a half liters of blood, or more than a third of her normal volume. It's not quite as bad as it sounds, because women's bodies bulk up on red blood cells, fluid, and clotting factors during pregnancy in evolutionary anticipation of blood loss. Still, Kopas, the doctor, and the nurse confer and decide to err on the side of caution and give Jones a blood transfusion.

Woozy from anemia and painkillers, Jones has been mostly quiet at the center of the medical whirlwind. Now she's starting to get worried. She has read about women bleeding to death and can't get the stories out of her mind. "I just need someone to tell me it's going to be OK," she says.

Kopas immediately sits next to Jones's bed and reassures her that the hospital is well-equipped to handle this kind of emergency. It's scary, but it's going to be fine. If Jones starts bleeding again, Kopas explains, she will have the obstetrician take charge. There's an array of surgical options, including a D&C and another procedure to close off damaged arteries by injecting them with tiny particles.

It never comes to that.

By 3:30 a.m., the crisis is past. Jones is stable and finally nodding off after more than twenty hours in the hospital. Kopas returns to her computer. Another midwife has come on duty, so Kopas could go home after she finishes charting the case. She doesn't even consider it. With the bed in the midwives' room occupied, she finds a spare bunk in the doctors' dorm. Kopas sets the alarm to go off every hour so she can check on her patient, then lies down to sleep.

The UW midwives attend about a third of the births at UW Medical Center–Northwest. That's three hundred babies a year, and the work never stops. Kopas is back in the clinic for another day of patient visits. Among the women on her schedule is Amie-June Brumble, who's coming in for a postpartum visit six weeks after delivering her second son.

Brumble and her husband named the baby Asher, which means "happy" and "blessed" in Hebrew. Asher is a little stuffed up from a respiratory bug, but he doesn't fuss as Brumble settles on the exam table and fills Kopas in on what's been going on since the birth.

The baby has been sleeping through the night—a luxury Brumble and her husband could only dream of with their firstborn. Big brother seems indifferent to the new arrival so far, but they're taking special care to keep him happy and head off resentment.

"Right," Kopas says. "You don't want him to be thinking, 'This baby showed up and suddenly there was no fun.'"

The women laugh and riff about sibling psychology before Kopas gets down to business.

"Physically, are you feeling OK?" she asks. "Are you feeling recovered?"

The answer is yes. Brumble is still bleeding a bit, but nothing major. The cramping is gone, and the sutured vaginal tear doesn't hurt anymore.

"How was the birth for you?" Kopas asks.

"I thought it went great," Brumble says. "The lead-up was a lot slower than I expected, then things started speeding up and that was nice."

"You were awesome," Kopas says.

"So were you," Brumble replies. "And the nurses. I felt like I was really well taken care of."

Kopas queries Brumble about her bowel movements, urination, and nipples. She suggests the couple continue to hold off on sex until the bleeding has stopped. They discuss postpartum depression. "If you're feeling like things aren't right, you can always talk to us about it," Kopas says.

While Brumble undresses, Kopas takes Asher into the hall to show him off. "We fight over holding babies around here," she says, cradling the little boy in her arms. He looks alarmed and balls up his fists but doesn't cry.

In a midwives' office, an infant is an irresistible draw. Staff gather and coo, admiring Asher's blue eyes and quilted white jammies decorated with little bears. No one flinches when he starts spitting up milky goo. Kopas grabs a cloth and cleans his face. "So looking at me made you throw up?" she says. "Did you overfill the belly just a little bit? It's OK. It happens."

Back in the exam room, she tucks Asher into his carrier and checks Brumble's breasts, pelvic area, and uterus. Everything looks good.

Brumble and her husband don't plan to have any more kids, so she and Kopas probably won't see each other again on a professional basis. But they're connected in a way neither will ever forget. The story of their second son's birth is one Brumble and her husband will cherish and retell for years to come. Asher was the 388th baby Kopas has caught since becoming a midwife. She may not recall the details of every delivery, but she always remembers the people.

As the exam draws to a close, Brumble and Kopas smile and wish each other well.

Kopas leaves the room, and Brumble gathers up her baby and baby gear, then heads to her car.

In the clinic hallway the midwife picks up the next chart and flips through the pages.

Another woman is waiting for her in exam room three.

ACKNOWLEDGMENTS

It would be impossible to write about midwifery without being able to observe midwives delivering babies. But when I started this project, I had no idea whether anyone would agree to having a journalist in the room during such an intensely intimate event.

So thank you, Amie-June Brumble, Stephanie Kaydus, and Jessica Jones (and your incredible partners), for sharing your birth experiences. It was an honor to be present when Asher, Savanna, and Samuel entered the world.

Huge thanks also to Mary Lou Kopas, who was enthusiastic from the start and let me shadow her for months; and to Ann Olsen, who gave me honey and introduced me to the world of home birth.

Tara Lawal, Faisa Farole, and their colleagues at Rainier Valley Midwives are doing amazing work, and I was lucky to get a glimpse of it. Many, many other midwives—some quoted in these pages, some not—educated me and shared their expertise and insights.

Susan Gregg, director of media relations for UW Medicine, opened the door. Barbara Clements, also with UW Medicine, spent her birthday and wedding anniversary with me—instead of with her family—waiting for babies to be born.

I'm also grateful to Mary Lou's colleagues at the UW Medical Center–Northwest midwifery group, who made me feel welcome and accommodated disruptions with good cheer.

Credit for the idea goes to Emily Simonson, of Simon & Schuster, who provided guidance and gentle editing. Peg Haller provided expert copyediting.

And finally, thanks to Patti Epler—a true friend and an excellent editor.

APPENDIX

The first step in becoming a midwife is to decide what kind of midwife you want to be and where you want to practice: in a hospital, in homes, in birth centers, or a combination. Because regulations vary so widely, an important second step is understanding the rules in the state where you intend to work.

The most versatile route into the profession is through nurse-midwifery, which requires a nursing credential and a graduate degree, and generally allows you to practice in any setting. Certified nurse-midwives (CNMs) can be licensed in every state, but some states—like California and Missouri—require them to be supervised by, or collaborate with, a physician. Other states, like Texas and Kentucky, limit their authority to prescribe medications. In Nebraska, CNMs are not allowed to oversee home births.

A second route, called direct-entry, is available for those who intend to specialize exclusively in home and birth center birth. Direct-entry midwives are not nurses, but most complete a three-year educational program.

As of early 2020, thirty-three states offer a pathway to licensure for direct-entry midwives, who can also be credentialed as certified professional midwives. Some states, like Nebraska, specifically outlaw nonnurse midwives. Others have no specific regulations, creating a gray area. States spell out the scope of practice for direct-entry midwives, including what medications they are allowed to administer during and after birth.

DEFINITIONS AND EDUCATIONAL PATHWAYS

Certified Nurse-Midwife: A registered nurse with a graduate degree in midwifery from a program accredited by the Accreditation Commission for Midwifery Education. CNMs must pass the certification exam of the American Midwifery Certification Board. They are licensed as advanced practice registered nurses (APRN), sometimes called advanced registered nurse practitioners (ARNP).

Nurse-midwifery is the most common path to becoming a midwife, and CNMs can be licensed in every state.

Many candidates earn a bachelor of science degree in nursing and become registered nurses before applying to a graduate program in midwifery. But many schools now offer an accelerated, one-year nursing program for students who have degrees in other fields. Some schools also combine undergraduate nursing and graduate nurse-midwifery education in a single program.

The midwifery education itself is generally a two- to three-year program leading to either a master's or doctoral degree. All programs include a mix of classroom education and clinical experience. In 2020, there were thirty-eight accredited nurse-midwifery education programs nationwide. Many offer distance-learning options ranging from coursework that is mostly online to hybrid models.

The majority of CNMs work in hospitals. In all but a few states, they are also authorized to attend births at home and in freestanding birth centers. CNMs can prescribe medications and offer full primary care to women throughout their lives, not just during pregnancy and childbirth. In 2020 there were about 13,000 CNMs, with nearly 700 new graduates a year. Mean/median annual salary estimates for CNMs range between $102,000 and $130,000.

The American College of Nurse-Midwives (ACNM) is the professional organization that represents CNMs.

Certified Midwife: A midwife who meets all the requirements for a CNM, except being a registered nurse. The credential was introduced by the ACNM in 1994 to open midwifery to people who did not want to earn nursing degrees, but it remains a rare pathway into the profession. In 2019 the ACNM estimated there were only about one hundred CMs practicing nationwide. The scope of practice for CMs is generally the same as for CNMs. State regulations determine the settings where CMs can work, including attending births at home, in birth centers, and in hospitals. As of 2020, CMs can be licensed in six states: Delaware, Hawaii, Maine, New York, New Jersey, and Rhode Island.

Direct-entry Midwife: A midwife who is not a nurse. Most have out-of-hospital practices and are sometimes called community midwives. The certification for most direct-entry midwives is certified professional midwife. Some states require certification for licensure, some do not.

Certified Professional Midwife: A direct-entry midwife who specializes in home and birth center births. The CPM credential is issued by the North American Registry of Midwives. There are two pathways to certification, both of which require passing a national certification exam.

Most new CPMs complete a three-year program accredited by the Midwifery Education and Accreditation Council. As of

March 2020, there were nine accredited programs nationwide. All offer a combination of classroom education and clinical training. Many are distance-learning programs.

An alternative, though increasingly unusual, pathway is via what's called a portfolio evaluation process, which is essentially an apprenticeship with an experienced midwife.

CPMs specialize in caring for women during pregnancy and birth, and in caring for newborns in the first few weeks of their lives. They are generally allowed to administer specific drugs during and after birth, but do not have prescribing authority. With very few exceptions, CPMs do not have hospital privileges.

There are about three thousand CPMs in the United States. Salary data is spotty, but one analysis estimates a mean income of about $50,000 in Washington State.

The certifying body for CPMs is the North American Registry of Midwives. The professional organization is the National Association of Certified Professional Midwives. Another professional and advocacy organization is the Midwives Association of North America, which is open to all types of midwives.

Licensed Midwife: A direct-entry midwife licensed to practice in a particular state. Requirements and scope of practice vary widely.

Lay Midwife: A term with many interpretations and no clear definition. Licensed midwives in some states are referred to as lay midwives. Some midwives who practice without a formal education or licensure call themselves lay midwives.

MIDWIFERY AND RELATED ORGANIZATIONS

The American College of Nurse-Midwives is the professional and advocacy organization for certified nurse-midwives and certified midwives.

The Midwives Alliance of North America is a professional organization open to all midwives. It advocates for midwifery and coordinates research.

The National Association of Certified Professional Midwives is the professional and advocacy organization for certified professional midwives.

The National Black Midwives Alliance supports black midwives and works to increase their numbers.

Sister Song is an organization that advocates for reproductive justice.

The International Confederation of Midwives supports, represents, and works to strengthen professional associations of midwives throughout the world.

US Midwifery Education, Regulation, & Association
is a coalition of organizations focused on midwifery
education, certification, accreditation, regulation,
association, and practice.

Childbirth Connection, founded in 1918 as the Maternity
Center Association, is a core program of the National
Partnership for Women & Families and a consumer
advocacy organization that collects and disseminates
evidence about safe, high-quality maternity care.

FURTHER READING

The Midwife: A Memoir of Birth, Joy, and Hard Times (2002) by
Jennifer Worth

A gritty memoir about midwifery care in London's
East End during the post–World War II baby boom and
the early days of the UK's National Health Service. The
book was the basis of the popular BBC television series
Call the Midwife.

Baby Catcher: Chronicles of a Modern Midwife (2002) by Peggy
Vincent

Entertaining and poignant birth stories spanning
the 1960s to early 1990s in California, by the first

independent nurse-midwife granted hospital privileges in the state.

Listen to Me Good: The Life Story of an Alabama Midwife (1996) by Margaret Charles Smith and Linda J. Holmes

An oral history from legendary Alabama midwife Margaret Charles Smith, who was ninety-one when she related stories from nearly five decades delivering babies in the rural South.

Delivered by Midwives: African American Midwifery in the Twentieth-Century South (2018) by Jenny M. Luke

An academic examination of the role of African American midwives, along with efforts to train, educate, and regulate them—and eventually force them out of practice.

Nurse-Midwifery: The Birth of a New American Profession (2006) by Laura E. Ettinger

A detailed account of the birth of nurse-midwifery and its evolution.

Spiritual Midwifery (1976, fourth ed. 2002) by Ina May Gaskin

The book that launched a thousand midwifery careers. A how-to manual, interspersed with stories of (mostly) hippie births, and advice for midwives and expectant mothers.

Birth Matters: A Midwife's Manifesta (2011) by Ina May Gaskin
> An update of the state of midwifery and the role of the midwifery model of care in the modern medical world, by a spiritual leader of the modern midwifery movement.

A History of Midwifery in the United States: The Midwife Said Fear Not (2016) by Helen Varney and Joyce Beebe Thompson
> A detailed academic and administrative history of nurse-midwifery and the many individuals and organizations central to its development and expansion.

A Midwife's Tale: The Life of Martha Ballard, Based on Her Diary, 1785–1812 (1990) by Laurel Thatcher Ulrich
> The Pulitzer Prize–winning story of a hardworking New England midwife, with historical context about politics, economics, medicine, and the role of women in the early United States.

Mary Breckinridge (2008) by Melanie Beals Goan
> The story of the Frontier Nursing Service of rural Kentucky and the founding of nurse-midwifery education in the United States.

Varney's Midwifery, 6th Ed (2019) edited by Takoa King, Mary Brucker, Kathryn Osborne, & Cecilia Jevitt
> The classic textbook of nurse-midwifery

Lying-In: A History of Childbirth in America (1977) by Richard
W. Wertz and Dorothy C. Wertz

A scholarly but engagingly written history that traces
the shift from birth as a natural event that occurred at
home to the medicalized vision of birth that prevails
today. Includes a good overview of efforts to wipe out
midwives.

FILM

The Business of Being Born

A 2008 documentary directed by Abby Epstein and
produced by actress Ricki Lake. The film is critical of
the standard way of giving birth in American hospitals,
explores the financial forces at work, and documents
alternatives, particularly home birth.

The Mama Sherpas

Produced by Ricki Lake and Abby Epstein and
directed by Brigid Maher, this 2015 documentary focuses
on collaborations between midwives and doctors to
reduce C-section rates.

SOURCES

CHAPTER 2

National Center for Health Statistics. *National Vital Statistics Report* 67 (8), Nov. 7, 2018.

Martin, Nina. "A Larger Role for Midwives Could Improve Deficient U.S. Care for Mothers and Babies." *ProPublica*, Feb. 22, 2018.

Stephenson, Jo. "Only half of babies in England now delivered by midwives." *Nursing Times*, Nov. 15, 2016.

"Maternal Mortality," "Pregnancy Mortality Surveillance System," Centers for Disease Control and Prevention. https://www.cdc.gov/reproductivehealth/maternal -mortality/index.html, accessed March 10, 2020.

GBD 2015 Maternal Mortality Collaborators. "Global, regional, and national levels of maternal mortality, 1990–2015: A systematic analysis for the Global Burden of Disease Study 2015." *Lancet* 388 (2016): 1775–812.

Vedam, Saraswathi, et al. "Mapping integration of midwives across the United States: Impact on access, equity, and outcomes." *PLOS ONE*, Feb. 21, 2018. https://doi .org/10.1371/journal.pone.0192523.

Souter, V., et al. "Comparison of Midwifery and Obstetric Care in Low-Risk Hospital Births." *Obstetrics & Gynecology* 134 (5): 1056–1065. Nov. 2019. doi: 10.1097 /AOG.0000000000003521.

Attanasio, Laura B., et al. "Midwife-led care and obstetrician-led care for low-risk pregnancies: A cost comparison." *Birth*. Nov. 2019. https://doi.org/10.1111/birt.12464.

CHAPTER 3

Cassidy, Tina. *Birth: The Surprising Story of How We Are Born*. New York: Grove Press, 2006.

"Babinden," Wikipedia, https://en.wikipedia.org/wiki /Babinden, accessed March 10, 2020.

Vilela, Alyssa. "Midwifery in Jamaica." Medium, Dec. 11, 2018, accessed March 10, 2020. https://medium.com/midwifery -around-the-world/midwifery-in-jamaica-c7bd2de7a9bc.

Giladi, Avner. "Liminal craft, exceptional law: Preliminary notes on midwives in medieval Islamic writings."

International Journal of Middle East Studies 42 (2010), 185–202. doi:10.1017/S0020743810000012.

Costa, Leopoldo. "Midwives and Maternity Care in the Roman World." *Stravaganza*, Feb. 19, 2012. https://stravaganzastravaganza.blogspot.com/2012/02/midwives-and-maternity-care-in-roman.html, accessed March 2020.

Iimura, Brett. "History of Midwifery in Japan." *Midwifery Today* 114, Summer 2015. https://midwiferytoday.com/mt-articles/history-of-midwifery-in-japan/.

Dawley, Katy, and Linda V. Walsh. "Creating a More Diverse Midwifery Workforce in the United States: A Historical Reflection." *Journal of Midwifery & Women's Health* 61, no. 5 (Sept. 2016): 578–85. doi:10.1111/jmwh.12489. Epub Aug 10, 2016.

Green, Monica H. "The Sources of Eucharius Rösslin's 'Rosegarden for Pregnant Women and Midwives' (1513)," *Med Hist* 53, no. 2 (April 2009): 167–92. doi:10.1017/s0025727300000193.

Ehrenreich, Barbara, and Deirdre English. *Witches, Midwives and Nurses: A History of Women Healers*, 2nd ed. New York: The Feminist Press at CUNY, 2010.

Roper, Lyndal. *Witch Craze: Terror and Fantasy in Baroque Germany*. New Haven: Yale University Press, 2006.

Epstein, Randi Hutter. *Get Me Out: A History of Childbirth from the Garden of Eden to the Sperm Bank*. New York, London: W. W. Norton & Company, 2010.

Ulrich, Laurel Thatcher. *A Midwife's Tale: The Life of Martha Ballard, Based on her Diary, 1785–1812*. New York: Knopf, 1990.

Gelbart, Nina. *The King's Midwife: A History and Mystery of Madame du Coudray*. Oakland, CA: University of California Press, 1999.

Wertz, Richard W., and Dorothy C. Wertz. *Lying-In: A History of Childbirth in America*. New Haven and London: Yale University Press, 1989.

Wilson, Adrian. *The Making of Man-Midwifery*. Cambridge, MA: Harvard University Press, 1995.

Linet, Martha S., et al. "Children's Exposure to Diagnostic Medical Radiation and Cancer Risk: Epidemiologic and Dosimetric Considerations." *Pediatr Radiol* 39, Suppl 1 (Feb. 2009): S4.

Declercq, Eugene, and Richard Lacroix. "The Immigrant Midwives of Lawrence: The Conflict Between Law and Culture in Early Twentieth-Century Massachusetts." *Bulletin of the History of Medicine* 59, no. 2 (Summer 1985): 232–46.

Luke, Jenny M. *Delivered by Midwives: African-American*

Midwifery in the Twentieth-Century South. Jackson, MS:
University of Mississippi Press, 2018.

Drife, J. "The Start of Life: A History of Obstetrics."
Postgraduate Medical Journal 78 (2002): 311–15.

CHAPTER 4

Goan, Melanie Beals. *Mary Breckinridge: The Frontier Nursing
Service and Rural Health in Appalachia.* Chapel Hill, NC:
University of North Carolina Press, 2012.

Dye, Nancy Schrom. "Mary Breckinridge, The Frontier
Nursing Service and the Introduction of Nurse-
Midwifery in the United States." *Bulletin of the History of
Medicine* 57, no. 4 (Winter 1983): 485–507.

Ettinger, Laura E. "Midwives on Horseback: Saddlebags and
Science." National Museum of American History, March
26, 2015. https://americanhistory.si.edu/blog/midwives
-horseback-saddlebags-and-science, accessed March 2020.

————. *Nurse-Midwifery: The Birth of a New American Profession.*
Columbus, OH: Ohio State University Press, 2006.

Wertz, Richard W., and Dorothy C. Wertz. *Lying-In: A History
of Childbirth in America.* New Haven and London: Yale
University Press, 1989.

Varney, Helen, and Joyce Beebe Thompson. *A History of Midwifery in the United States: The Midwife Said Fear Not*. New York: Springer Publishing Company, 2016.

Schultz, Gladys Denny. "Cruelty in Maternity Wards." *Ladies' Home Journal*, May 1958, p. 44.

Epstein, Randi Hutter. *Get Me Out: A History of Childbirth from the Garden of Eden to the Sperm Bank*. New York, London: W. W. Norton & Company, 2010.

Caton, Donald. "Who Said Childbirth Is Natural?: The Medical Mission of Grantly Dick-Read." *Anesthesiology* 84 no. 4 (1996): 955–64.

Day, Beth. "The Return of the Midwife." *Redbook*, March 1969.

CHAPTER 5

Gaskin, Ina May. *Spiritual Midwifery*, 4th ed. Book Publishing Company: 2002

CHAPTER 6

Patel, I., J. Chang, et al. "Patient satisfaction with obstetricians and gynecologists compared with other specialties: Analysis of US self-reported survey data." *Patient Related*

Outcome Measures 2 (2011), 21–26. https://doi.org/10.2147
/PROM.S15747.

Carter, Analiesse, MD, and Natalie Nunes, MD. "In low-
risk pregnant women in labor, does continuous fetal
heart monitoring lead to improved maternal and
perinatal outcomes compared to intermittent fetal heart
rate auscultation?" *Evidence-Based Practice* 22, no. 12
(December 2019): 11–12, doi:10.1097
/EBP.0000000000000445.

CHAPTER 7

Kopas, Mary Lou. "A Review of Evidence-Based Practices for
Management of the Second Stage of Labor." *Journal of
Midwifery & Women's Health*, May 21, 2014. https://doi
.org/10.1111/jmwh.12199.

ACNM Fact Sheet. "Essential Facts about Midwives." https://
www.midwife.org/acnm/files/cclibraryfiles
/filename/000000007531/EssentialFactsAboutMidwives
-UPDATED.pdf, accessed March 2020.

Institute for Health Metrics and Evaluation (IHME).
"Financing Global Health 2018: Countries and Programs
in Transition." Seattle, WA: IHME, 2019.

Petersen, E. E., N. L. Davis, D. Goodman, et al. *"Vital Signs:* Pregnancy-Related Deaths, United States, 2011–2015, and Strategies for Prevention, 13 States, 2013–2017." *MMWR Morb Mortal Wkly Rep* 68 (2019): 423–29. http://dx.doi.org/10.15585/mmwr.mm6818e1external icon.

Gunja, Munira Z., et al. "What Is the Status of Women's Health and Health Care in the U.S. Compared to Ten Other Countries?" Commonwealth Fund, Dec. 19, 2018. https://www.commonwealthfund.org/publications/issue-briefs/2018/dec/womens-health-us-compared-ten-other-countries?omnicid=EALERT1531955&mid=alain.sherter@cbsinteractive.com, accessed March 2020.

GBD 2015 Maternal Mortality Collaborators. "Global, regional, and national levels of maternal mortality, 1990–2015." *Lancet* 388 (2016): 1775–812.

Centers for Disease Control and Prevention, Reproductive Health. "Severe Maternal Morbidity in the United States." https://www.cdc.gov/reproductivehealth/maternalinfanthealth/severematernalmorbidity.html, accessed March 2020.

National Center for Health Statistics. "Births—Method of Delivery." https://www.cdc.gov/nchs/fastats/delivery.htm, accessed March 2020.

World Health Organization. "WHO Statement on Caesarean

Section Rates." April 2015. https://www.who.int
/reproductivehealth/publications/maternal_perinatal
_health/cs-statement/en/, accessed March 2020.

United Health Foundation, America's Health Rankings.
"Infant Mortality." https://www.americashealthrankings
.org/explore/health-of-women-and-children/measure
/IMR_MCH/state/ALL, accessed March 2020.

Chen, Alice, et al. "Why Is Infant Mortality Higher in the
United States Than in Europe?" *Am Econ J Econ Policy*.
8, no. 2 (May 2016): 89–124. doi:10.1257/pol.20140224.

Centers for Disease Control and Prevention, Reproductive
Health. "Infant Mortality." https://www.cdc
.gov/reproductivehealth/maternalinfanthealth
/infantmortality.htm, accessed March 2020.

Rayburn, William F. *The Obstetrician-Gynecologist Workforce in the
United States: Facts, Figures, and Implications, 2017.* American
Congress of Obstetricians and Gynecologists, 2017.

CHAPTER 8

Goer, Henci. "Dueling Statistics: Is Out-of-Hospital Birth
Safe?" *Journal of Perinatal Education* 25, no. 2 (Spring,
2016): 75–79. http://dx.doi.org/10.1891/1058-1243.25.2.75.

Shah, Neel. "A NICE Delivery—The Cross-Atlantic Divide over Treatment Intensity in Childbirth." *New England Journal of Medicine* 372, no. 23 (June 4, 2015): 2181–2183.

Royal College of Obstetricians and Gynaecologists/Royal College of Midwives. "Home Birth." Joint Statement No. 2 (April 2007).

Committee on Obstetric Practice, American College of Obstetricians and Gynecologists. "Planned Home Birth." Committee Opinion no. 697 (April 2017). https://www .acog.org/-/media/project/acog/acogorg/clinical/files /committee-opinion/articles/2017/04/planned-home -birth.pdf, accessed March 2020.

National Center for Health Statistics. *National Vital Statistics Reports* 67 (8), Nov. 7, 2018.

MacDorman, Marian, and Eugene Declercq. "Trends and State Variations in Out-of-Hospital Births in the United States, 2004–2017." *Birth* 46, no. 2 (June 2019): 279–88. doi:10.1111/birt.12411.

Varney, Helen, and Joyce Beebe Thompson. *A History of Midwifery in the United States: The Midwife Said Fear Not.* New York: Springer Publishing Company, 2016.

Cheng, Yvonne, et al. "Selected perinatal outcomes associated with planned home births in the United States." *Am J Obstet Gynecol* 209 (2013): 325. e1-8.

Wax, J. R., et al. "Maternal and newborn outcomes in planned home birth vs. planned hospital births: a metanalysis." *Am J Obstet Gynecol* 203 (2010): 243. e1-8.

De Jonge, A., et al. "Perinatal mortality and morbidity in a nationwide cohort of 529,688 low-risk planned home and hospital births." *BJOG* 116 (2009): 1177–84.

Hutton, Eileen K., et al. "Perinatal or neonatal mortality among women who intend at the onset of labour to give birth at home compared to women of low obstetrical risk who intend to give birth in hospitals: A systematic review and meta-analysis." *J.eclinm* 14 (2019): 59–70. https://doi.org/10/1016.

Johnson, Kenneth C., and Betty-Anne Daviss. "Outcomes of planned home births with certified professional midwives: large prospective study in North America." *BMJ* 330 (7505): 1416. Jun 18, 2005. https://www.ncbi.nlm.nih.gov/pubmed/15961814, accessed April 2020.

Olsen, O., and J. A. Clausen. "Benefits and harms of planned hospital birth compared with planned home birth for low-risk pregnant women." *Cochrane*, Sept. 12, 2012.

Vedam, Saraswathi, et al. "Mapping integration of midwives

across the United States: Impact on access, equity, and outcomes." *PLOS ONE*, Feb. 21, 2018. https://doi .org/10.1371/journal.pone.0192523.

CHAPTER 9

National Center for Health Statistics. *National Vital Statistics Reports* 67 (8), Nov. 7, 2018.

Ernst, Kitty, and Kate Bauer. "Birth Centers in the United States." American Association of Birth Centers, 2017.

Varney, Helen, and Joyce Beebe Thompson. *A History of Midwifery in the United States: The Midwife Said Fear Not.* New York: Springer Publishing Company, 2016.

Brody, Jane. "Center for Childbirth—a Homelike Setting." *New York Times*, Sept. 15, 1975.

O'Donnell, Michelle. "A Birthing Center Falls Prey to Rising Insurance Costs." *New York Times*, Aug. 24, 2003.

Rooks, J. P., et al. "Outcomes of care in birth centers. The National Birth Center Study." *N Engl J Med* 321, no. 26 (Dec. 28, 1989): 1804–11.

Stapleton, Susan Rutledge, et al. "Outcomes of Care in Birth Centers: Demonstration of a Durable Model." *J Midwifery Women's Health* 58 (2013): 3–14.

Department of Health and Human Services; Centers for
    Medicare & Medicaid Services. "Strong Start for
    Mothers and Newborns Initiative." *Joint Information
    Bulletin*, Nov. 9, 2012; https://www.medicaid.gov
    /sites/default/files/federal-policy-guidance/downloads
    /cib110918.pdf, accessed March 2020.

CHAPTER 11

Nursing Practice Review: Midwifery. "Addressing
    psychological distress in midwives." *Nursing Times* 112,
    no. 8, Feb. 24, 2016: 22–23.
Leinweber, Julia, et al. "The costs of 'being with the woman':
    secondary traumatic stress in midwifery." *J.Midw.* 26, no.
    1, April 3, 2008. doi:10.1016.
Borritz, M., et al. "Burnout among employees in human
    service work: design and baseline findings of the PUMA
    study." *Scand J Public Health* 34, no. 1 (2006): 49–58.

CHAPTER 12

GBD 2015 Maternal Mortality Collaborators. "Global,
    regional, and national levels of maternal mortality,

1990–2015: A systematic analysis for the Global Burden of Disease Study 2015." *Lancet* 388 (2016): 1775–812.

Peterson, Emily E., et al. "Racial/Ethnic Disparities in Pregnancy-Related Deaths—United States, 2007–2016." *Morbidity and Mortality Weekly Report* 68, no. 35 (Sept. 6, 2019): 762–65.

Serbin, Jyesha Wren and Elizabeth Donnelly. "The Impact of Racism and Midwifery's Lack of Diversity: A Literature Review." *Journal of Midwifery & Women's Health* 61, no. 6 (Nov./Dec. 2016): 694–706. doi: 10.1111/jmwh.12572stiy.

Ettinger, Laura E. "Midwives on Horseback: Saddlebags and Science." National Museum of American History, March 26, 2015. https://americanhistory.si.edu/blog/midwives -horseback-saddlebags-and-science, accessed March 2020.

Varney, Helen, and Joyce Beebe Thompson. *A History of Midwifery in the United States: The Midwife Said Fear Not.* New York: Springer Publishing Company, 2016.

DeLibertis, Jodi. *Shifting the Frame: A Report on Diversity and Inclusion in the American College of Nurse-Midwives.* American College of Nurse-Midwives, 2015.

Accreditation Commission for Midwifery Education. "Midwifery Education Trends Report, 2019." American College of Nurse-Midwives, 2019.

CHAPTER 13

Muglu, Javaid, et al. "Risks of stillbirth and neonatal death with advancing gestation at term: A systematic review and meta-analysis of cohort studies of 15 million pregnancies." *PLoSMed* 16(7) (July 2, 2019). https://doi.org/10.1371/journal.pmed.1002838.

Grobman, William A., et al. "Labor Induction versus Expectant Management in Low-Risk Nulliparous Women." *N Engl J Med* 379 (2018) 513–23. doi:10.1056/NEJMoa1800566.

Callaghan, W. M., et al. "Trends in postpartum hemorrhage: United States, 1994–2006." *Am J Obstet Gynecol* 202, no. 4 (April 2010): 353.e1-6. doi:10.1016/j.ajog.2010.01.011.

APPENDIX

American College of Nurse-Midwives. "Comparison of Certified Nurse-Midwives, Certified Midwives, Certified Professional Midwives Clarifying the Distinctions among Professional Midwifery Credentials in the U.S." Oct. 2017. https://www.midwife.org/acnm/files/ccLibraryFiles/FILENAME/000000006807

/FINAL-ComparisonChart-Oct2017.pdf, accessed March 2020.

Smith, Brianna, and Renée Tomilla. "Washington State Certified Professional Midwives: Income and Practice Characteristics Survey." Master's thesis, Bastyr University, 2017.

ABOUT THE AUTHOR

Sandi Doughton is an award-winning science writer for *The Seattle Times* and the author of *Full Rip 9.0: The Next Big Earthquake in the Pacific Northwest*. Doughton has been covering science, health, and the environment in the Pacific Northwest for more than twenty years. She lives in Seattle, Washington.